C Programming with Solved Problems

P. Sojan Lal
Jeeva Jose
Edwin Basil Lal

ATLANTIC
PUBLISHERS & DISTRIBUTORS (P) LTD

Published by

ATLANTIC

PUBLISHERS & DISTRIBUTORS (P) LTD

7/22, Ansari Road, Darya Ganj, New Delhi-110002
Phones : +91-11-40775252, 40775214, 23273880, 23275880
Fax : +91-11-23285873
Web : www.atlanticbooks.com
E-mail : orders@atlanticbooks.com

Branch Office: Chennai
Phones : +91-44-48531784, 28291383
E-mail : chennai@atlanticbooks.com

Printed & bound in India by Atlantic Print Services

Preface

C is a general-purpose, high-level procedural language. It was designed to be compiled using a compiler to provide low-level access to memory, to provide language constructs that map efficiently to machine instructions and to require minimal run-time support. C is therefore useful for many applications that had formerly been coded in assembly language, such as in system programming. C has now become a widely used professional language for various reasons like being easy to learn, having a structured language, producing efficient programs, handling low-level activities and the ability of being compiled on a variety of computer platforms.

The language was designed to encourage cross-platform programming. A standards-compliant and portably written C program can be compiled for a wide variety of computer platforms and operating systems with a few changes to its source code. The language has become available on a very wide range of platforms—from embedded microcontrollers—to super-computers. C is extensively used for "system programming", including implementing operating and embedded system applications, due to a combination of desirable characteristics such as code portability and efficiency, ability to access specific hardware addresses and low run-time demand on system resources. C can also be used for Website programming using CGI as a "gateway" for information between the Web application, the server, and the browser. Some reasons for choosing C over interpreted languages are its speed, stability and near-universal availability.

One consequence of C's wide availability and efficiency is that compilers, libraries and interpreters of other programming languages are often implemented in C. The primary implementations of Python, Perl 5 and PHP are all written in C.

Due to its thin layer of abstraction and low overhead, C allows efficient implementations of algorithms and data structures, which is useful for programs that perform a lot of computations. For example, the GNU Multiple Precision Arithmetic Library, the GNU Scientific Library, Mathematica and MATLAB are completely or partially written in C.

C is sometimes used as an intermediate language by implementations of other languages. This approach may be used for portability or convenience; by using C as an intermediate language, it is not necessary to develop machine-specific code generators. C has some features, such as line-number preprocessor directives and optional superfluous commas at the end of initializer lists, which support compilation of generated code. C has also been widely used to implement end-user applications.

Chapter 1 of the book shares the fundamentals of C programming. Chapter 2 introduces the learner to C programming. The Control Statements are introduced in chapter 3, and Advanced Control Statements are covered in chapter 4. The Arrays are explained in chapter 5. Chapter 6 takes care of the functions. Chapter 7 goes into the details of String Handling. Chapter 8 gives detailed information on Structure & Union. Chapter 9 teaches about pointers. Files are explained in detail in chapter 10. The advanced topics in C, like typedefs, enumerated data types, command line arguments, macros and pre-processors are taken care of in chapter 11.

All chapters have worked out programs, illustrations, review, and frequently asked university questions. All the solved lab exercises in this book are tested and output provided.

The book will be useful for the students and teachers of computer science and professionals using C programming.

P. Sojan Lal
Jeeva Jose
Edwin Basil Lal

Contents

CHAPTER 1

C Programming Fundamentals

1.1 Introduction

Computer programming is the task of writing instructions for a computer, to solve any problem. The programmers use high level languages like C, C++, Java, FORTRAN, COBOL, Python, SQL and HTML for programming. Programming is actually interpretation of the algorithm in any high level language. The purpose of all these languages is to communicate between user and computer for the execution of certain task.

C is a programming language developed at AT&T's Bell Laboratories of USA in 1972. It was designed and written by Dennis M. Ritchie. Brain W. Kernighan and Dennis M. Ritchie first defined the C language in their book, *The C Programming Language* published in 1977. The American National Standards Institute (ANSI) set up a committee to define an official standard for C, in 1983. This version is referred as ANSI C or standard C. The programs written in C are simple, efficient and much faster due to its variety of data types and powerful operations.

Some popular versions of C compilers are:

Microsoft C Quick C
Turbo C Lattice C
Aztec C Borland C

C is a general-purpose high level programming language. Various implementations of C exist and many similarities between each one of them. This chapter introduces the basic concepts of C programming.

Learning C language is similar to learning English language, which you can experience in the following sections. Fig. 1.1 illustrates the methodology of learning English and C. Therefore, we start with character set of C language in the next section.

- Steps in learning English language

Alphabets → Words → Sentence → Paragraphs

- Steps in learning C language

Character set → Constants, Variables, Keywords → Statement → Program

Fig. 1.1: Methodology of learning English and C

1.2 The C Character Set

The following shows the valid character set in C. It consists of alphabets, digits and special symbols.

1. Alphabets A, B, C, ... X, Y, Z
   a, b, c, ... x, y, z
2. Digits 0, 1, 2, 3, 4, 5, 6, 7, 8, 9
3. Special Symbols ~ ' ! @ # % ^ & * ( ) _ - + =
   | \ { } [ ] : ; " ' < > , . ? /

1.3 Constants, Variables and Keywords

A proper combination of alphabets, numbers and special symbols makes constants, variables and keywords. Let us call the following box which represents a memory cell in a computer and may call it as A.

A | 2 8 4 |

Here 284 is a ***constant.*** The content of memory 'A' can be changed. 'A' is called a ***variable***, i.e., we can store another value in the same location by replacing the existing value 284.

1.4 Types of C Constants

The constants and variables in C are like constants and variables in Algebra. Consider the algebraic expression x + 2y + 3z. Here x, y, z can assume any value, but the coefficients 1, 2, 3 are fixed and remain unchanged. Quantities whose values do not change in a problem are known as constants and whose values change are known as variables. Similarly constants and variables are defined in C, but according to certain rules.

C constant can be divided into two major categories. Fig. 1.2 shows different types of C constants.

1. Primary constant
2. Secondary constant

C Constants	
Primary Constant	**Secondary Constant**
1. Integer Constant	1. Array
2. Real Constant	2. Pointer
3. Character Constant	3. Structure
	4. Union
	5. Enumerated, etc.

Fig. 1.2: Types of C constants

We shall see the details of primary constants in this chapter.

1.5 Rules for Constructing Integer Constant (or called Fixed Point Constants)

- An integer must have at least one digit.
- It must not have a decimal point.
- It could be either positive, negative or zero.
- Unsigned numbers are being treated as positive.
- No commas or blanks are permitted within an integer constant.
- The allowable ranges of integer constants are –32768 to 32767, for a 16-bit computer. Maximum integer value lies in the range of $-(2^{31}-1)$ to $(2^{31}-1)$.

Valid Integer Constants (Fixed Point Constants)

a. 23
b. –456
c. 0

Invalid Integer Constants

a. 23.	Decimal not permitted.
b. –45,6	Comma is not permitted.
c. 434 7	Blank space is not permitted.

1.6 Rules for Constructing Real Constant (or called Floating Point Constants)

- A real constant must have at least one digit followed by a decimal point.
- It must have a decimal point.
- It could be either positive, negative or zero.
- Unsigned numbers are being treated as positive.
- No commas or blanks are permitted within a real constant.

Valid Real Constants (or Floating Point Constants)

a. 23.0
b. –456.0
c. 0.0
d. +565.78

Invalid Real Constants

a. 23. Two digits before dot are not permitted.
b. –45,6.0 Comma is not permitted.
c. 434 7.0 Blank space is not permitted.

1.7 Rules for Constructing Character Constant

- A character constant is a single alphabet, a single digit or a special character enclosed in single inverted commas. Both the inverted commas should point to left. Hence, '9' is a valid character constant and ‘9’ is not a valid character constant.
- The maximum length of a character constant is one.

1.8 Types of C Variables

Variables are used in C for storing constants in various memory locations. The type of the variable and type of the constant should be the same. It means that, only integer constant can be stored in an integer variable, real constant can be stored in a real variable and character constant can be stored in a character variable. The type of constant accepted depends on each programming language.

1.9 General Rules for Constructing Variable Names (Identifiers)

- The first character of a variable name must be an alphabet.
- Upper and lower case letters are different.
- The remaining characters of variable name can be alphabet, digit or underscore. The length of variable is restricted to 8, even though some compilers may allow maximum 40 characters.
- No commas, blanks or special characters except underscore are allowed.

Valid Real Variable Names

- a
- amount
- sum

- mark_ttl
- mark_avg
- age

Invalid Variable Names

- average mark Use of blank space is not permitted.
- total.mark Use of decimal is not permitted.
- student.id Use of decimal is not permitted.

Rules for a variable name apply to primary and secondary variables. It is mandatory to declare all types of variables explicitly at the beginning of a program so that the compiler distinguishes the variable type at the beginning itself. Type declaration statement is as follows:

```
int studt_id, mark1, mark2, ttl_mark;
float area, radius, avg_mark;
char flag;
```

The naming of variable names shall be meaningful as far as possible. The content of the variable should be known unambiguously from the name of the variable itself, as above.

Note: However, this practice of naming variables shall be altered for certain larger software projects to minimize software piracy. The scope of such software obfuscation techniques to mislead the pirates is outside the scope of this introductory programming book. We shall be practicing the conventional variable naming techniques as illustrated above throughout this book to convey easy program logic.

1.10 C Keywords

Keywords are also called reserved words in C language. These keywords have assigned meaning by C compiler and it is recommended not to use these keywords as variable names or symbolic constants. Some compilers may allow using keywords as variable names. The following identifiers are reserved for use as keywords, and may not be used otherwise. Fig. 1.3 shows list of keywords in C.

auto	break	case	char
const	continue	default	do

double	else	enum	extern
float	for	goto	if
int	long	register	return
short	signed	sizeof	static
struct	switch	typedef	union
unsigned	void	volatile	while
			packed

Fig. 1.3: List of Keywords in C

Note: Some implementations also reserve *fortran* and *asm*. The keywords const, signed, and volatile are new with the ANSI standard.

1.11 Symbolic Constants

Symbolic constants are used to define a fixed value for a variable which will not change during the execution of a program. For example, the value of PI which is approximately equal to 3.14. In certain cases, you may require further accuracy for PI. Then this variable has to be replaced in many places of the program, that is you have to explicitly change at all the places for the correct result. Moreover, symbolic constants are useful to have certain meaning in program coding. For instance, when you write 40, it does not mean anything more than an integer 40. But when you write MAX_TEMP, STUD_NOS, PAS_MARK, etc. are assigned to a symbolic constant and thus it becomes meaningful. Hence, we use such variables, called symbolic constants to represent certain constants in many occasions. This can be achieved by defining symbolic constants as shown below in C.

```
#define MAX_TEMP 40
#define LOW_TEMP 25
#define PI 3.14
#define XMAX 5
```

1.12 Data Types

In C programming language, data types refer to an extensive system used for declaring variables or functions of different types. The type of a variable determines how much space it occupies in storage and how the bit pattern stored is interpreted.

The types in C can be classified as follows:

1. Basic types. They are arithmetic types and consist of the two types: (a) integer types and (b) floating-point types.
2. Enumerated types. They are again arithmetic types and they are used to define variables that can only be assigned certain discrete integer values throughout the program.
3. The type void. The type specifier void indicates that no value is available.
4. Derived types. They include (a) Pointer types, (b) Array types, (c) Structure types, (d) Union types, and (e) Function types.

The array types and structure types are referred to collectively as the aggregate types. The type of a function specifies the type of the function's return value. We will see basic types in the following section, whereas, other types will be covered in the upcoming chapters.

Integer Types

Following table gives you details about standard integer types with its storage sizes and value ranges:

Type	Storage size	Value range
char	1 byte	-128 to 127 or 0 to 255
unsigned char	1 byte	0 to 255
signed char	1 byte	-128 to 127
int	2 or 4 bytes	-32,768 to 32,767 or -2,147,483,648 to 2,147,483,647
unsigned int	2 or 4 bytes	0 to 65,535 or 0 to 4,294,967,295
short	2 bytes	-32,768 to 32,767
unsigned short	2 bytes	0 to 65,535

long	4 bytes	-2,147,483,648 to 2,147,483,647
unsigned long	4 bytes	0 to 4,294,967,295

To get the exact size of a type or a variable on a particular platform, you can use the *sizeof* operator. The expressions *sizeof* (type) yields the storage size of the object or type in bytes. Following is an example to get the size of int type on any machine:

```
#include<stdio.h>
#include<limits.h>
void main()
{
  printf("Storage size for int : %d \n",
  sizeof(int));
  getch();
}
```

When you compile and execute the above program it produces the following result on windows:

```
Storage size for int : 2
```

Floating Point Types

Following table gives you details about standard floating point types with storage sizes and value ranges and their precision.

Type	Storage size	Value range	Precision
float	4 byte 3.4E+38	1.2E-38 to	6 decimal places
double	8 byte 1.7E+308	2.3E-308 to	15decimal places
long double	10 byte	3.4E-4932 to 1.1E+4932	19 decimal places

The Void Type

The void type specifies that no value is available.

1.13 C Statements

- ✓ Type declaration statement: declares type of variables used in the program.
- ✓ Input/output statement: for inputting data to the program and getting output/result.
- ✓ Arithmetic statement: performs arithmetic operations for constants and variables.
- ✓ Control statement: controls the sequence of execution of various program statements. Sequence control, decision control, loop control and case control statements are the various control statements.

We shall discuss about the type declaration statement in this chapter. The input/output statement and arithmetic statements are explained in detail in the next chapter to follow. Control statements are described in Chapter 3.

1.14 Type Declaration Statement

All variables used in a program must be declared before using them in a program. Type declaration statement is usually used at the beginning of C program. Each statement ends with a semi-colon.

```
int age, score;
float avg_mark, interest, gravity;
char name, bar_code;
```

1.15 Summary

We have introduced fundamental parts of C programming—constants, variables, keywords, data types and type declaration statement. We have seen integer, floating point, character constants and variables.

1.16 Review Questions

1. Describe the methodology of learning C.
2. Name few compilers of C.
3. List down some keywords in C.
4. Classify types of constants in C.

5. Describe rules for constructing integer and floating point constants.
6. What are the uses of symbolic constants? Give examples for symbolic constants in C.
7. Explain different data types used in C.
8. Explain with examples identifiers and keywords in C.
9. What are user defined data types?

CHAPTER 2 C Program—Introduction

2.1 Introduction

This chapter introduces simple C programs. Relevant flowcharts, programs and its output are given for easy understanding of the algorithm and result of program execution. All the given programs are tested and executed. However, we do not take guarantee of the results on your machine.

2.2 Executing a C Program

C programs are written in a file by giving a name with a ".c" extension name. Executing a C program follows the following pattern. We need to make sure that the written program is error free to execute it. The program can be made error free by a process called *compilation*. This is done with the help of any C compiler. The compiler will check the program for error; if successful it will create an *object file* with ".obj" extension. This object file will contain the object program, which can be linked with libraries to generate an *executable file* with ".exe" extension. This .exe file is used for running the program. Fig. 2.1 shows the steps to execute a C program.

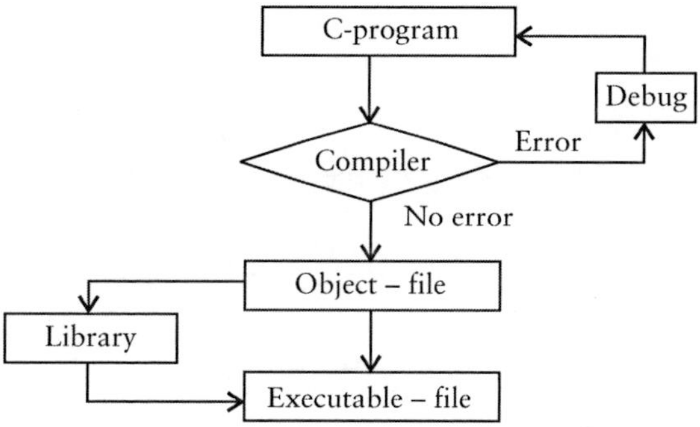

Fig. 2.1: Steps to execute a C Program

The *C standard library* consists of a collection of headers and library routines used to implement common operations, such as input/output and string handling, in the programming language C. If there are any errors in the program during compilation, the errors will be reported to the user. User then has to correct the error and carry out the same steps to execute the program and the process is known as debugging.

2.3 Input/Output Statements

C does not directly provide input/output statements and no built in file access methods exist. These are provided as library functions. Input and output statements are used for reading and writing the data to and from the program. To illustrate these will see our first C program and the flowchart is shown in Fig. 2.2. This program will print a message "Welcome to the Disney land".

Program 2.1

```
Line 1: /* Program to print Welcome to the
Disney land */
Line 2: #include <stdio.h>
Line 3: void main()
```

```
Line 4: {
Line 5: printf("Welcome to the Disney land. \n");
Line 6: }
```

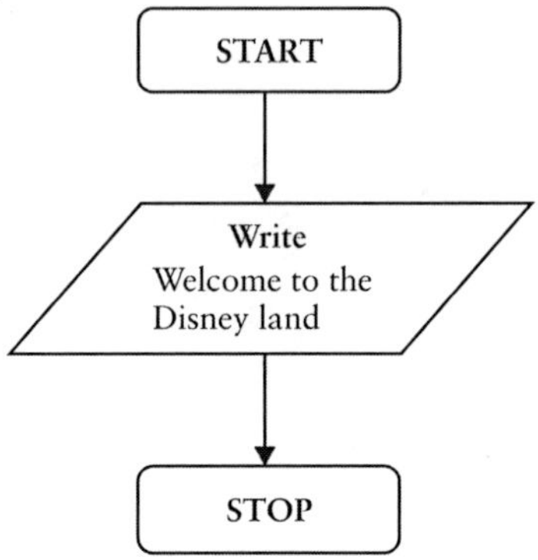

Fig. 2.2: Flowchart to print a message

Our first C program contains six lines. We will discuss all these six statements in detail. The first line /* Program to print Welcome to the Disney land */ is a C comment. Any character between /* and */ are ignored by the compiler. This can be used for documenting a program thus makes easier to understand. The second line

```
#include<stdio.h>
```

tells the compiler to include information about the standard input/output library. This library contains procedure to print values from the program to the output device and to get the values to the program from an input device. (Use ^F1 in turbo C and see help to find details of the header files.)

All C programs consist of functions. Each function is intended for certain tasks. This is similar to subtasks in a major project. In a programming paradigm, we often subdivide any major tasks into one or more sub programs called function. Every C program must have at least one function name "main" from which the execution of the program always starts. So the second line

```
void main()
```

defines a function named “main” which has no arguments,[1] indicated by empty list (). Normally, any name can be given to function, but “main” is a special function. This means that every program must have a “main” somewhere.

The statements of a function are enclosed in braces {} and these constitutes the body of the function. The opening ‘{’ and closing ‘}’ braces are used to identify the start and end of the function.

The line

```
printf("Welcome to Disney land. \n");
```

is a function statement inside the “main” function. Note that, a function, by its name, followed by a parenthesized list of arguments. In this example, the argument to the printf function is the sequence of character “Welcome to Disney land. \n”. printf is a library function that prints sequence of characters, in this case the string of characters between the quotes. Note that all executable and nonexecutable statements in C end with a semicolon.

The ‘\n’ in the quoted string is C notation for the ‘new line character’, which is used to advance the output printing to the left margin on the next line. Note that ‘\n’ is an escape sequence and is single character. Few other escape sequence characters are ‘\t’ for tab, ‘\b’ for back space, ‘\’ for double quotes and ‘\\’ for the back slash.

2.4 Variables and Arithmetic Expressions

All programming languages normally use *variables* to store data in RAM during execution of a program. The name of an employee, company number, social security number, date of birth, date of joining, married or not, number of dependents, name of dependent, salary and sex are few examples of data relevant to an employee. All these can be stored in computer using *variables* of different *types*. Salary shall normally be an *integer* whereas the name of an employee is a *text* (sequence

1. *sin(x)* is a pre-defined function in C to evaluate the *sine* series. Here *x* is the argument and *sin* is the function name. Similarly, *sqrt(y)* is another pre-defined function to find the square root where *sqrt* is the function name and *y* is the argument.

of alphabets and numbers). The company number could be a combination of alphabets and integers like a passport number (ex. AA143256). Therefore, company number can be treated as a text.

Let us see another program to discuss this topic.

Program 2.2 Draw a flowchart and write a C program to store 15 and 24. Find their sum and then print the result.

```
#include<stdio.h>
void main()
{
  int i,j,sum;
  i = 15;
  j = 24;
  sum = i + j;
  printf("%d %d %d ",
i,j,sum);
}
```

Declare variables as integer

Output

```
15 24 39
```

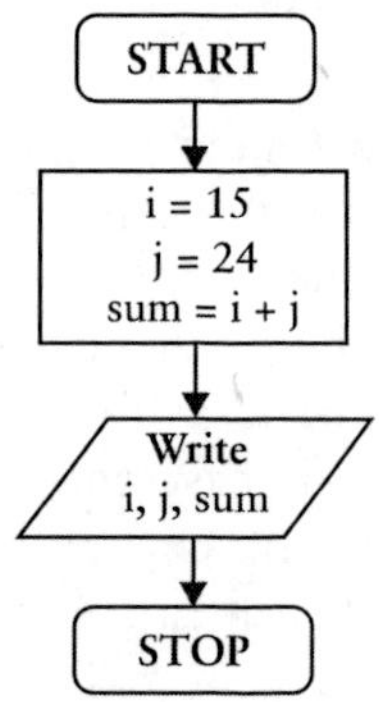

Fig. 2.3: Flow Chart to find sum of two numbers

In this program, we are using three *variables* i, j and sum. The variables are used to store data in memory location. Computer internally will have a decoded representation for variables, which is called memory address. Note that in C, all variables have to be declared before they are used, conventionally in the beginning of the function main before any executable statements. The line

```
int i,j,sum;
```

is a declaration statement. A *declaration* declares the variables used in the program, however, it does not hold any value at this time. It also declares some properties of that variable. Here, 'int' declares a property called *type*. The type 'int' means that the variables i, j, sum are integers and thus can hold only integer values.

2.4.1 The Assignment Statements

```
i = 15;
j = 24;
```

set the variables i and j to hold the values 15 and 24 respectively. This is also called as defining the variables, since we are setting with the initial values. Just for the purpose of illustration, you may refer to Fig. 2.4.

Value	Address
15	0000(i)
24	0001(j)
39	0010(sum)
..	..
..	..

Fig. 2.4: Simple Memory Representation

Here each variable i, j and sum will have one to one representation to each of the cells memory as shown in Fig. 2.4.

The line

```
sum = i + j;
```

contains an **arithmetic expression** "i + j". Here, since the arithmetic operation is sum denoted by '+' sign, values of variables i and j are summed. The result, here it is 39, will be assigned to the variable sum.

The next line in this example shows a bit more of how *printf* works. Its first argument is a string of characters to be printed, with each '%' indicating which argument is to be substituted, and in what form it is to be printed. For instance, '%d' specifies an integer argument. Second, third and fourth arguments are i, j and sum respectively. So the statement

```
printf("%d %d %d",i,j,sum);
```

causes the values of the integer variables to be printed. Note that, the argument substitution is by the order of the position of variables. First '%' will be substituted with the value of first integer variable i, second '%' with the second integer variable j, so on. That is, they must match up properly by number and type; otherwise you will get wrong answer.

To say a limitation of this program, one needs to modify the program every time, if we need to work it with different values for i and j. The next program explains how to overcome this limitation.

Program 2.3 Draw a flowchart and write a program to find the sum of any two given integers.
Hint: The value of two variables i, j is given through the keyboard.

```
#include<stdio.h>
void main()
{
  int i,j,sum;
  printf("Input two integers
\n");
  scanf("%d %d",&i,&j);
  sum = i + j ;
  printf("%d %d %d
\n",i,j,sum);
}
```

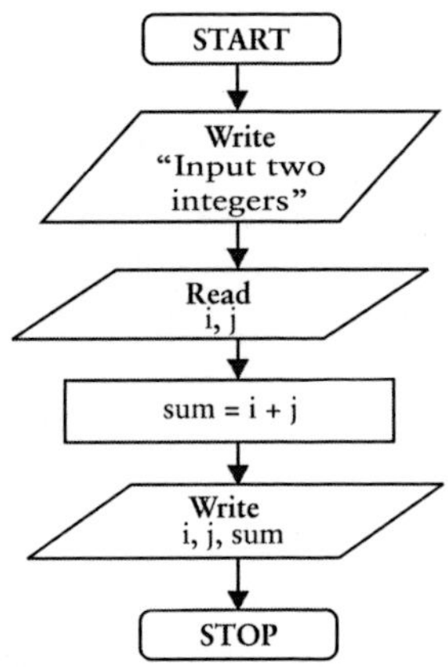

Fig. 2.5: Flowchart to find the sum of any two integers

Output

```
Input two integers
32 24 <Press Enter>    Keyboard Entry
32 24 56
```

This program is as same as the previous program, but a line of statement that needs attention is

```
scanf("%d %d",&i,&j);
```

The function *scanf* reads input values from standard input, interprets them according to the specification format, and stores them in memory. The first argument specifies the control string. The control string specifies the field format of the input values. That is, the conversion character '%' followed by the type of data that is to be assigned to the variables. Here, both '%d' specifies that the input values must be interpreted and assigned as an integer value. Next arguments is the address of the location, specified using '&', of the variables (here variable 'i' & 'j') where the read values is to be stored.

Input/output formatting will be discussed in the coming topics.

2.4.2 Arithmetic Statements

An arithmetic statement in C resembles like a mathematical formula. An arithmetic statement has Left Hand Side (LHS), Right Hand Side (RHS) and an equality symbol in between. The LHS must be a variable name while the RHS is an expression containing as many sub-expressions and variables as required.

The general form (called syntax) of an arithmetic statement is

Variable = Expression

The following are some simple valid arithmetic expressions. We shall discuss about other types of expressions in the forth coming chapters.

*0.5 * base * height*

(a + b + c)/2.0

x − y

Here a, b, c, x, y, base and height are called variables and *, /, + and − are called arithmetic operators.

These arithmetic expressions can be assigned to a variable as follows to make a valid arithmetic statement in C. The result of the RHS will be stored in the memory location of the variable on LHS.

*area = 0.5 * base * height;*

perimeter = a + b + c;

difference = x − y;

A semi-column separator is used in C at the end of each statement. It is preferred to use only one statement in each line as a best programming practice. This will increase the readability of the program.

When a statement is executed, the value of the expression on the RHS is first evaluated, and then the result is stored as new value of the variable on the LHS. This implies that all variables on the right hand side of an arithmetic statement must have some value assigned to it, before the execution of the statement. All the above given programs have followed this simple rule. Now let us see a valid arithmetic statement.

perimeter = a + b + c;

s = perimeter/2.0;

Here the initial value of the variable perimeter is calculated in the first statement and the same value is then substituted in the second statement. The above two statements can be combined to a single statement as follows:

s = (a + b + c)/2.0;

Before proceeding further, we must know certain fundamental rules in programming called precedence rule. The precedence rules in C are detailed in Table 2.1.

The evaluation of an arithmetic expression starts from left to right. All expressions inside a parenthesis have the highest precedence. Then the multiplication and division has equal precedence in the order of appearance. Addition and negation has got the least precedence in an arithmetic expression.

We shall see the following pair of examples to understand the significance of a precedence rule. The step by step execution of the arithmetic statements is shown below.

With the above examples, we have noticed that the computer first evaluates the expression within parenthesis, followed by multiplication and division and then followed by addition and subtraction, from left to right. Hence, extreme care should be taken while writing the C statements. The following examples illustrates further.

(Let a = 2, b = 3, c = 4, d = 5)

Table 2.1: Precedence Rules

sum = a + b * c; = 2 + 3 * 4 = 2 + 12 = <u>14</u>	sum = (a + b) * c; = (2 + 3) * 4 = 5 * 4 = <u>20</u>
sum = a + b * c – d; = 2 + 3 * 4 – 5 = 2 + 12 – 5 = <u>9</u>	sum = (a + b) * (c – d); = (2 + 3) * (4 – 5) = 5 * (–1) = <u>–5</u>
sum = d – c / a + 2 * b; = 5 – 4 / 2 + 2 * 3 = 5 – 2 + 6 = <u>9</u>	sum = (d – c) / a + 2 * b; = (5 – 4) / 2 + 2 * 3 = 1 / 2 + 2 * 3 = 0.5 + 6 = <u>6.5</u>

Let a = 2, b = 3, c = 4, d = 5

1. sum = (a + b) * c;
   = (2 + 3) * 4 — Execution within parenthesis
   = 5 * 4 — Multiplication
   = <u>20</u>
2. sum = (a + b) * (c – d);
   = (2 + 3) * (4 – 5) — Execution within parenthesis
   = 5 * (–1) — Multiplication
   = <u>–5</u>
3. sum = d – c / a + 2 * b;
   = 5 – 4 / 2 + 2 * 3 — Multiplication and division from L->R
   = 5 – 2 + 6 — Addition and subtraction from L->R
   = <u>9</u>
4. sum = (d – c) / a + 2 * b;
   = (5 – 4) / 2 + 2 * 3 — Execution within parenthesis
   = 1 / 2 + 2 * 3 — Multiplication and division L->R
   = 0.5 + 6 — Addition
   = <u>6.5</u>

2.5 Input/Output Formatting

One of the essential operations performed in a C language programs is to provide input values to the program and output the data produced by the program to a standard output device. Even though we have studied its essentials, number of formatting specifications are provided with these functions, and will discuss in detail here.

2.5.1 Input Statement

This statement is used for inputting data to the program. One of the common input statements in the C program is *scanf*. *scanf* reads characters from the standard input, interprets them according to the specifications in format, and stores the results through the remaining arguments. The *scanf* function has the general form

scanf ("control string", arg1, arg2, arg3............, argn);

The general format for reading a integer number is

scanf("%xd",&a); where

percent sign (%) denotes the conversion character specifier

x is the format conversion modifier (optional). This is an integer number which specifies the width of the field of the number that is being read.

d is a conversion character. It specifies the type of data that is to be assigned to variable of the assignment, here it is integer.

a is a variable to be read by the program. Table 2.2 shows the basic scanf conversions.

Table 2.2: Basic scanf Conversions

Character	Input Format
d	decimal integer.
i	integer (may be in octal (leading 0), or hexadecimal (leading 0x or 0X).
o	octal integer (with or without a leading zero).
x	hexadecimal integer (without a leading 0x 0X)
u	unsigned decimal integer.

c	characters. The next input characters (default 1) are placed at the indicated spot in memory.
s	character string (not quoted).
e, f, g	floating point number with optional sign, optional decimal point, and optional exponent.
%	no argument is converted.

Example

The following examples show how the formatting is done using *scanf* while reading the data

(1) scanf("%d%d%d",&a,&b,&c);

In this scanf statement, a, b and c are integer variables whose values is to be read by using '%d' format which is to be used for integer variables. The data values are supplied from the data screen using the following pattern

10 20 30

The output is a = 10, b = 20 and c = 30

(2) scanf("%d%f%g",&a,&b,&c);

In this case, we see that a is integer variable but b and c are float variables. Format given for a is d, but for b it is f (for accepting decimal points) and for c format given is g (for accepting exponent). Now the data value supplied is

10 2.36 2.0e5

The output is a = 10, b = 2.36, c = $2.0*10^5$

(3) scanf("%5d%5d%5d",&a,&b,&c);

In this case, every thing is same as the first example except we have added format conversion modifier with modifier 5 which means that 5 spaces are to be reserved for reading of values of a, b and c. Now the data supplied from the screen will be

10 20 30

Here we see that the variables a, b and c are provided with five spaces.

2.5.2 Output Statement

This statement is used for formatted output printing such as variables, text, etc. The general form of the statement is

printf ("format specifier", argument list);

The general format for printing a integer number is

printf ("%xd",y);

where

percent sign (%)	–	denotes the conversion character specifier
x	–	is the format conversion modifier (optional). This is an integer number which specifies the width of the field of the number that is to be printed.
d	–	is a conversion character. It specifies the type of data that holds in the variable 'y', here it is integer.
y	–	is a variable to be printed by the program.

The format string contains two types of objects: ordinary text, which are copied as it is to the output, and conversion specifications, each of which can, use to format and print the next successive argument to printf. Each conversion specification begins with a % and ends with a conversion character. Between the % and the conversion character there may be, in order:

- A minus sign, which specifies left adjustment of the converted argument.
- A number that specifies the minimum field width. The converted argument will be hinted in a field at least this wide. If necessary it will be padded on the left (or right, if left adjustment is called for) to make up the field width.
- A period, which separates the field width from the precision.

- A number, the precision, that specifies the maximum number of characters to be printed from a string, or the number of digits after the decimal point of a floating point value, or the minimum number of digits for an integer.
- An h if the integer is to be printed as a short:, or l (letter ell) if as a long
- Conversion characters are shown in Table 2.3.

Table 2.3: Basic printf Conversion Characters

Character	Argument Type;	Printed As
d, i	int;	decimal number.
O	int;	unsigned octal number (without a leading zero).
x, X	int;	unsigned hexadecimal number, using lower case a-z or using upper case A-Z.
U	int;	unsigned decimal number.
C	int;	single character.
S	char *;	print string.
F	double;	print float value.
e, E	double;	print float value in exponential form.
g, G	double;	print using %e or %f whichever is smaller.

Example

If the variables a = 10, b = 20 and c = 30, then the

(1) printf ("%d %d %d",a,b,c);

will print: 10 20 30

(2) printf ("5% %5d %5d",a,b,c);

will print: 10   20   30

(3) printf ("d = %d\n",b+c);

will print: d = 50

Next we will see some programs

Program 2.4 Draw a Flowchart and write a program to find the area and perimeter of a triangle.

```
#include<stdio.h>
#include<math.h>
void main()
{
  float peri,area,a,b,c,s;
  printf("Enter the lengths.\t");
  scanf("%f %f %f", &a, &b, &c);
  peri = a + b + c;
  s = peri / 2.0 ;
  area = sqrt(s*(s-a)*(s-b)*(s-c));
printf("Area:%5.2f&Perimeter:
%5.2f\n",area,peri);
}
```

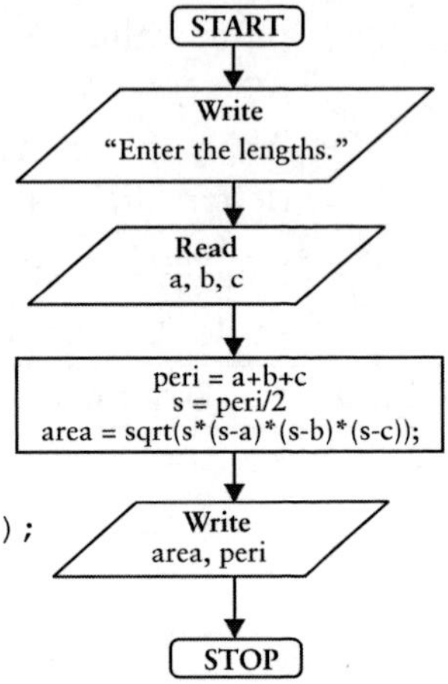

Fig. 2.6: Flowchart to find the area and perimeter of a triangle

Output

```
Enter the lengths.
3 4 5 <CR>
Area: 6.00 & Perimeter:12.00
```

#include <math.h> is included in the above program 2.4 to evaluate the square root function *sqrt*.

Program 2.5 Draw a flowchart and write a program for temperature conversion from degree Fahrenheit to degree Celsius. Hint: c = 5 * (f-32) / 9

```
#include<stdio.h>
void main()
{
  float f,c;
  printf("Input the value of
  F. \n");
  scanf("%f", &f);
  c = 5 * (f-32) / 9;
```

```
  printf("F = %4.1f C =
  %4.1f",f,c);
}
```

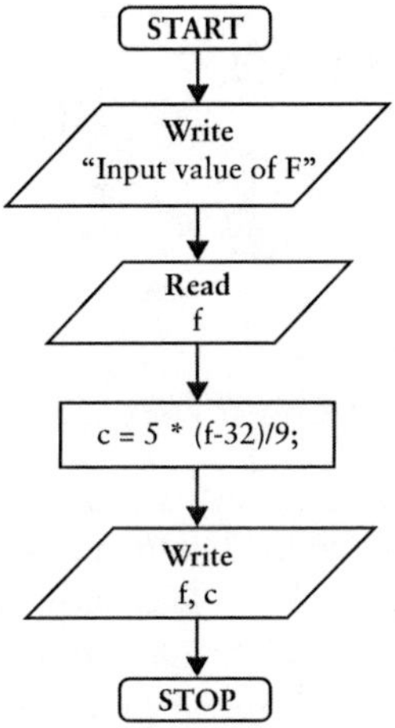

Fig. 2.7: Flowchart to calculate Degree C

```
Input the value of F.    ← First run.
32                       ← Data input
F = 32.0 C = 0.0         ← Output
Input the value of F.    ← Second run
70                       ← Data input
F = 70.0 C = 21.1        ← Output
```

2.6 Summary

We have seen some simple C programs with its equivalent flowcharts. The sequence of execution of the program is from top to bottom. However, we can alter the sequence of execution by using control statements, which is described in the next chapter to follow.

2.7 Review Questions

1. Write a simple output statement in C to print your name.
2. What are the uses of variables?
3. Describe printf and scanf functions.
4. Draw a flowchart and write a program to find the area of a rectangle whose sides are a and b.
5. List and explain various format field specifications of scanf statements. Give examples and explain their meanings.

CHAPTER 3

Introduction to Control Statements

3.1 Introduction

The sequence of execution of statements in a program can be altered as desired by using conditional (*if, nested if, if else* and *else if*) statements. It is required for decision-making. The following constructs are available in C for conditional branching.

1. *if* statement.
2. *if-else* statement.
3. *if-else-if* statement.

Before we begin to study about the control statements, it is essential to understand relational and arithmetic operators.

3.2 Relational and Arithmetic Operators

The six *relational operators* in C are < > <= >= (less than, greater than, less than or equal to, greater than or equal to) with the same precedence and the *equality operators* ==, != (equal to, not equal to). The equality operators have precedence just below the formerly mentioned four *relational operators*. All these six *relational operators* have lower precedence than the *arithmetic operators* (*, /, +, –). Multiplication and division operators have high precedence compared to addition and subtraction operators. We have already observed some simple precedence rules in Section 2.4 with examples. Table 3.1 illustrates the precedence and associativity of operators. Unary +, – and * have higher precedence than the binary forms.

Table 3.1: Precedence and Associativity of Operators

Operators	Description	Associativity
( )	Function call	Left to right
[ ]	Array subscript	
.	Structure member	
->	Pointer to structure member	
++	Post-increment	
—	Post-decrement	
!	Negation	Right to left
~	One's compliment	
++	Pre-increment	
—	Pre-decrement	
+	Unary plus	
-	Unary minus	
*	Indirection	
&	Address of	
(type)	Typecast	
sizeof	sizeof	
* / % and modulus	Arithmetic multiply, divide	Left to right
+ -	Arithmetic add and subtract	Left to right
<< >>	Left and right bit shift	Left to right
< <= > >=	Relational	Left to right
= = !=	Relational	Left to right
&	Bitwise AND	Left to right
^	Bitwise XOR	Left to right
|	Bitwise OR	Left to right
&&	Logical AND	Left to right

<table>
<tr><td>||</td><td>Logical OR</td><td>Left to right</td></tr>
<tr><td>?:</td><td>Conditional</td><td>Right to left</td></tr>
<tr><td>=</td><td>Assignment</td><td></td></tr>
<tr><td>+= -= *= /=
%= &= ^= |=
<<= >>=</td><td>Compound Assignment</td><td>Right to left</td></tr>
<tr><td>,</td><td>Comma</td><td>Left to right</td></tr>
</table>

3.3 *if* Statement

Conditional branching (decision-making) can be achieved by using ***if*** statement. It is a two-way decision-making statement used in conjunction with an expression. The expression is evaluated first and then the decision is taken based on the value of the expression, i.e. true (non-zero value) or false (zero value).

Note that by Fig. 3.1, the execution flow, *Statement*$_1$ followed by *Statement*$_2$ or *Statement*$_2$ alone, will be depending on the value of the expression. When the expression is non-zero (true), both statements, *Statement*$_1$ and *Statement*$_2$ will be executed, otherwise the control comes directly to *Statement*$_2$. That is, no matter whether the expression is *true* or *false*, *Statement*$_2$ will definitely execute.

Usually, the expression in an *if* statement is a relational, equality, or logical expression, but as the syntax shows, an expression from any domain in permissible.

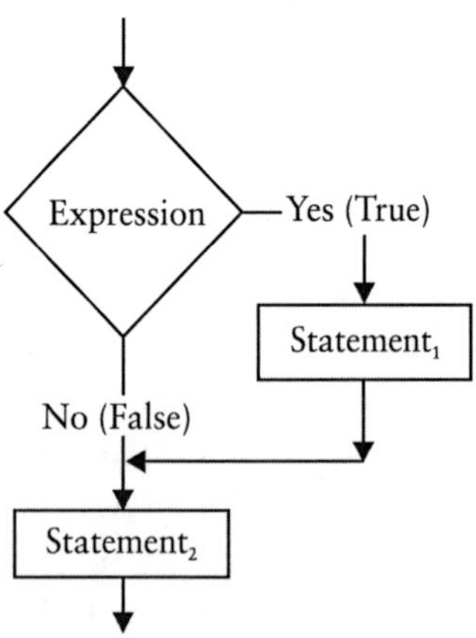

Syntax in C
if (expression)
Statement$_1$
Statement$_2$

Fig. 3.1: Flowchart for *if* statement

Example

Program 3.1 Program segment illustrating *if* statement.

```
big = a;
if(b > big)
        big = b;
printf("The big number is %f \n", big);
```

1. Initially the value of variable '*a*' is assigned to the variable '*big*'.
2. When the value of the expression '*b* > *big*' is true *big* = *b* will be executed.
3. Now the variable '*big*' will have the biggest value and its value will be printed.

The above ***if*** statement can be replaced by a *conditional expression* using a *conditional operator* (also known as *ternary operator)* "?:", which has three operands. It has a general form

$$\text{expression}_1 \ ? \ \text{expression}_2 \ : \ \text{expression}_3$$

the expression *expression*$_1$ is evaluated first. If it is non-zero (true), then the expression *expression*$_2$ is evaluated, and this will be the value of the conditional expression. Otherwise *expression*$_1$ is evaluated and now that becomes the value. Only one of *expression*$_2$ and *expression*$_3$ is evaluated.

Then the above ***if*** statement can be rewritten using *conditional expression* like this

big = (a>b) ? a:b;

It should be noted that the *conditional expression* is indeed an expression; it can be used as similar to any other expressions.

By considering the above *if* statement, the *Statement*$_1$ can be a single or a compound statement. The compound statements are enclosed in a pair of braces {}, as shown in the following program segment to make it as a single block. Here when the given number is above 100 it gives an increment to the counter, *count*, and prints the current value of variable 'a'. Both statements are enclosed in braces. The conditional construct *if* can be looped (repeated) as desired by using any of the looping constructs.

```
count = 0
............
............
if (a > 100)
{
  count = count + 1;
  printf("The number %f is above 100 \n", a);
  }
..............
..............
printf("Total numbers above 100 is %d \n",
count);
```

3.4 *if-else* Statement

We may have to specify the second branching in many applications, i.e. a set of statements will be executed only when the expression is *false*. The ***if-else*** statement is for doing that. Either *statement*$_1$ or *statement*$_2$ execute depends on the value of the expression as shown in Fig. 3.2.

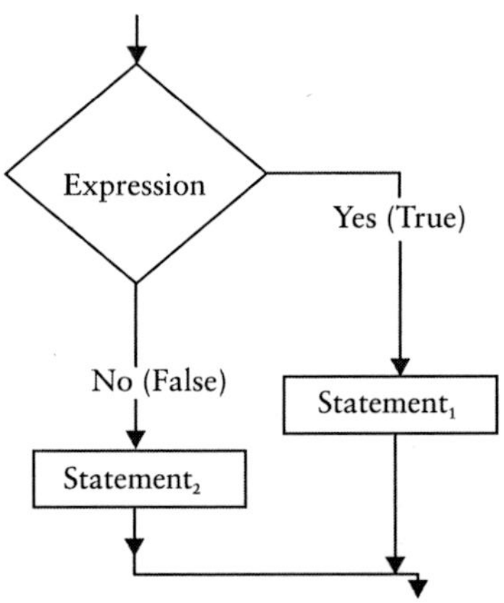

Syntax
if (expression)
Statement$_1$
else
Statement$_2$

Fig. 3.2: Flowchart for *if-else* statement

Program 3.2 Program to find the largest number, using floating point variable.

```
#include<stdio.h>
void main()
{
 float a,b;
 scanf(“%f %f”,a,b);
 if(a>b)
     printf(“%f greater
 than %f \n”, a,b);
 else
     printf(“%f greater
 than or equal to %f
 \n”, b,a);
}
```

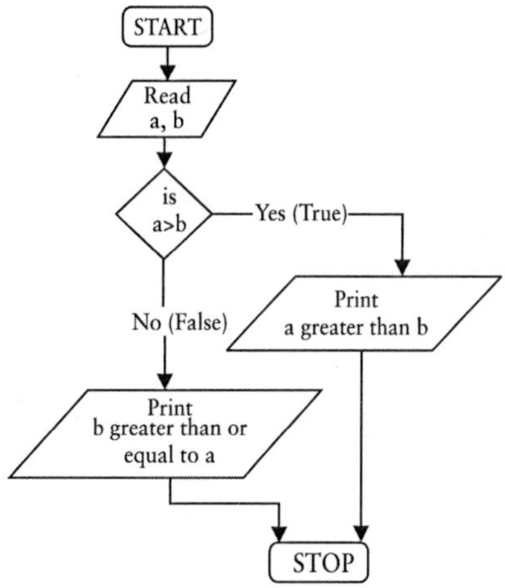

Fig. 3.3: Flowchart for finding biggest of two numbers

Output

```
20.1 7.2

20.1 greater than 7.2
```

3.5 *if-else-if* Statement

When *expression*$_1$ has non-zero (true) value, *statement*$_2$ will be executed, if not the program checks the condition of *expression*$_3$ and so on. If all the three expressions have zero value (false) then the default *statement*$_4$ will be executed. This is also known as *if-else ladder*. Fig. 3.4 illustrates an *if-else ladder.*

Syntax

if (**expression**$_1$) else if (**expression**$_2$)
 Statement$_1$ Statement$_2$
else if (**expression**$_3$)else
 Statement$_3$ Statement$_4$

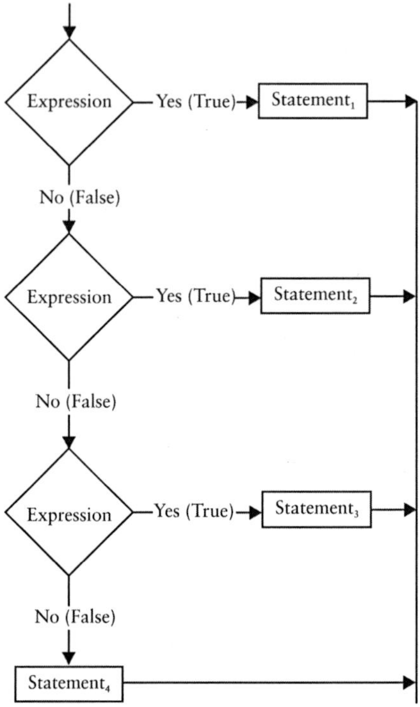

Fig. 3.4: Flowchart for *if-else-if* statement

If any expression is true, then statement associated with it is executed and this terminates the whole chain. The last *else* part handles the "none of the above" or default case where none of the other conditions are satisfied. Sometimes there is no explicit action for the default; in that case the trailing

```
else
    Statement4
```

can be omitted, or it may be used for error checking to catch a totally unexpected (or impossible) condition.

3.6 Nested *if* Statement

This type of statement is used when there are two or more decisions are to be made before the execution and these decisions are interdependent. In this, the *if* statements are nested together and the decisions are made after evaluating these conditions

Consider an example

```
if (n > 0)
if (a > b)
        big = a;
else
        big = b;
```

3.6.1 Dangling *else* Problem

The above program causes an ambiguity to the compiler. That is, it is not clear from the code that to which *if* statement, the *else* is associated with. This code illustrates the ***dangling else problem.*** This ambiguity is resolved by the compiler, by associating *else* with the nearest *if*.

So from the above example, the *else* goes with the inner *if*. If that is not what you want, braces must be used to force the proper association.

```
if (n > 0)
{
        if (a > b)
                big = a;
}
else
        big = b;
```

3.7 Solved Programs

Program 3.3 Program to find the roots of a quadratic equation for all the three different values (-ve, zero and +ve) of *disc*.

```
#include<stdio.h>
#include<math.h>
void main()
{
 float disc, a, b, c, root1, root2, root;
printf("Enter 3 values a, b, c:");
scanf("%f %f %f",&a, &b, &c);
 disc = (b*b - 4 * a * c);
```

```
  if(disc==0)
  {
      root = -b/(2 * a);
        printf(“Equal root %f \n”, root);
  }
  else
  if(disc < 0)
      printf(“Imaginary root \n”);
  else
  {
      root1=(-b+sqrt(disc)) / (2*a);
      root2=(-b-sqrt(disc)) / (2*a);
      printf(“Roots:%f,%f\n”,root1,root2);
    }
  }
```

Output

```
Enter 3 values a, b, c: 2 9 1
Roots:-0.113999, -4.386001
```

Program 3.4 Write a C program to find the area and perimeter of a rectangle.

```
#include<stdio.h>
#include<math.h>
void main()
{
  float peri, area, length, breadth;
  printf(“Enter the length and breadth.\t”);
  scanf(“%f %f ”, &length, &breadth);
  peri = 2* (length + breadth);
  area = length * breadth; printf(“Area:%5.2f&Peri
meter:%5.2f\n”,area,peri);
}
```

Output

```
Enter the length and breadth.
4 5 <CR>
Area: 20.00 & Perimeter:18.00
```

Program 3.5 Write a C program to find whether a given number is odd or even. If even, print its square root.

```
#include
#include<stdio.h>
#include<math.h>
void main()
{int n;
float s;
printf(“Enter a number: ”);
scanf(“%d”,&n);
if(n%2==0){
printf(“The number %d is even\n”,n);
printf(“The square root of %d is %f”,n,sqrt(n));
}
else
printf(“The number %d is odd”,n);
}
```

Output

```
Enter a number:5
The number 5 is odd
```

Program 3.6 Write a program to determine if a year is leap year or not

```
#include<stdio.h>
void main()
{
 int year;
 printf(“Enter a year to check if it is a leap
year\n”);
 scanf(“%d”, &year);
 if ( year%400 == 0)
 printf(“%d is a leap year.\n”, year);
 else if ( year%100 == 0)
 printf(“%d is not a leap year.\n”, year);
 else if ( year%4 == 0 )
```

```
printf("%d is a leap year.\n", year);
else
printf("%d is not a leap year.\n", year);
getch();
}
```

Output

```
Enter a year to check if it is a leap year
    2015
    2015 is not a leap year.
```

3.8 Summary

We learned to transfer the sequence of program execution using various control statements in C like *if*, *if-else*, *nested if*, etc. We shall study the details of advanced control statements in next chapter to follow.

3.9 Review Questions

1. What is precedence rule?
2. Explain simple *if* with an example.
3. Explain *if-else* with an example.
4. Explain *nested if* with an example.
5. Explain various relational and arithmetic operators.
6. Describe with suitable examples, all the operators in C; specify their hierarchy operators.

CHAPTER 4

Advanced Control Statements

4.1 Introduction

In the previous chapter, we have seen how the conditional statements (*if, nested if, if else* and *else if*) shall be used to alter the decisions by given conditions. In this chapter, we will study more advance statements in C language to change the control of the program.

Advanced control statements that are available in C can be categorized into following:

- ✓ branching (*switch* and *case*)
- ✓ looping (*for, while,* and *do-while*)
- ✓ jumping (*continue, break, goto* and *return*)

It is required for decision-making, repeating the loop for finite and infinite number of times, multiple branching and making time delay during program execution. We shall see the following constructs of C in this chapter.

1. *for* loop
2. *while* loop

3. *do-while* loop
4. *switch-case* statement
5. *goto* statement

4.2 *for* and *while* Loops

Generally, both *for* and *while* looping constructs are used for executing a group of statements iteratively. These two control loops are nearly identical for the purpose and used interchangeably in almost all applications. It is primarily a matter of personal preference for the selection of *for* or *while* loop.

The general form of *for* statement and its flowchart is given in Fig. 4.1. There are three components in a *for* statement separated by a semicolon (;) and each components are expressions. Most commonly *expression*$_1$ and *expression*$_3$ are assignment statement or a function call, while *expression*$_2$ is a relational expression. The operation of *for* statement is as follows:

Syntax

for (expression$_1$; expression$_2$; expression$_3$) statement;

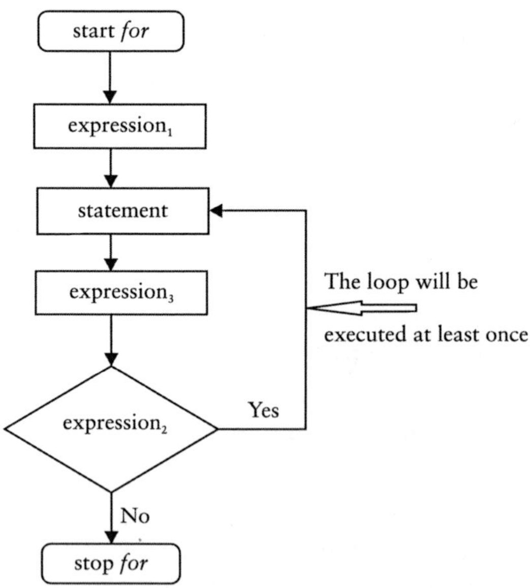

Fig. 4.1: Flowchart of *for* loop

It starts with the *expression*$_1$. Normally, this will be an initialization statement. Then it executes the statements (body of *for* loop). After finishing executing the statements, it calculates *expression*$_3$. Then a condition check performs between *expression*$_2$ and *expression*$_3$. It performs the execution of statements repeatedly until the condition becomes false. It should be noted that the loop will be executing at least once.

Any of the three components of *for* loop can be omitted, although the semicolon must remain. If *expression*$_1$ or *expression*$_3$ omitted, it will becomes only a conditional check loop.

```
i=0;  sum=0;
for( ;  i<=10;  )
{
        i  =  i  +  1;
        sum  =  sum  +  i;
}
```

As a special case, when *expression*$_2$ is missing, then the condition in the *for* loop is always true, i.e. an infinite loop.

```
i=0;  sum=0;
for( ;  ;  )            infinite  loop
{
        i  =  i  +  1;
        sum  =  sum  +  i;
}
```

for loop is used if we have a pre-knowledge about how many times the loop must be iterated. If not, the better choice is while loop. The general form and flow chart of *while* loop is given in Fig. 4.2. The loop will be executed only after evaluating the value of expression$_2$.

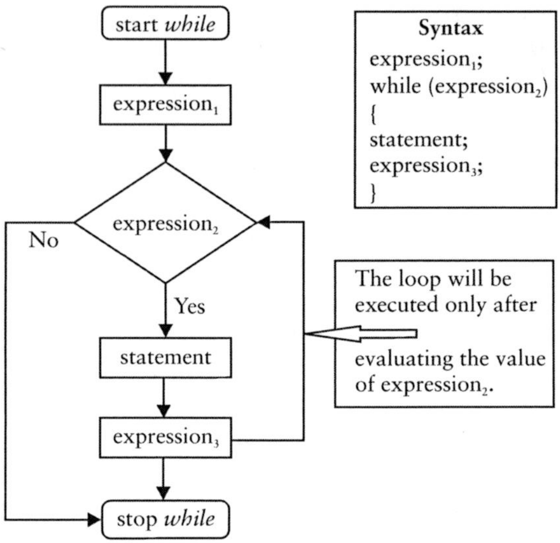

Fig. 4.2: Flowchart of *while* loop

We shall see some programs with the above looping statements.

Program 4.1 Write a program to find the sum of first 100 integers. Show the intermediate results.

```
#include<stdio.h>
/* Program to find the sum of first 6 integers with
intermediate results. */
void main()
{
  int i,sum=0;
  for ( i=1; i <= 6 ; i = i + 1)
  {
      sum = sum + i;
      printf("%3d %5d \n", i,sum);
  }
}
```

Note: *sum* is declared and initialised to zero in the declaration part itself. The index 'i' initialized to 1. The terminating condition i<=6, checks by the loop. For incrementing the index of the loop i by 1, i = i +1 is used. \n is used in *printf* for a new line as discussed earlier.

Output

```
1 1
2 3
3 6
4 10
5 15
6 21
```

Program 4.1.1 Let us see the following program for finding the sum and average of the given three real numbers for an infinite set of data.

```
#include<stdio.h>
 void main()
{
   float a,b,c,sum,avg;
   while (scanf("%f %f %f", &a, &b, &c) !=
EOF)
   {
          sum = a + b + c;
          avg = sum /3;
          printf("Sum is %f & Average %f",
sum,avg);
   }
}
```

/* Another version of the above program using *goto* statement is shown in Section 4.5 */

The body of *while* loop will be executed till you enter ^Z (holding down the control key press "z") or F6 (function key 6) for EOF (represents End Of File) followed by <CR> [carriage return]. The *scanf* recognize the EOF and terminates the loop. You are advised to execute the program and see the execution of the infinite loop till you enter EOF.

Program 4.2 Write a program to find the square and cube of first 4 integers.

```
#include<stdio.h>
void main()
{
 int i,sqr,cube;
```

```
  for(i=1; i <= 4 ; i= i+1)
  {
  sqr = i * i ;
  cube = i * i * i;
  printf("%2d %2d %2d \n",i,sqr,cube);
}
}
```

```
1   1   1
2   4   8
3   9  27
4  16  64
```

Table 4.1: Examples of *for* Loop and its Equivalent *while* Loop

	for loop	*while* loop

Program 4.1.1	`for(i =0, i<100; i++)`
	`sum = sum + i;`
		`i = 0;`
		`while(i<100)`
		`{`
		` sum = sum + i;`
		` i++;`
		`}`

Program 4.1.2	`for (i = 0, j = 0;`
	`i <100; i++, j = j+2)`
	`sum = sum + i + j;`
		`i = 0; j=0;`
		`while(i<100)`
		`{ i = i +1;`
		`j= j+2;`
		` sum = sum + i +j;`
		`}`

Program 4.1.3	`#include<stdio.h>`
	`void main()`
	`{`
	` int i,j,sum=0;`
	` for (i =100, j=0;`
	` j < i; i = i+1,`
	` j = j+2)`
	`  sum = sum + i + j;`
		`#include<stdio.h>`
		`void main()`
		`{`
		`int i=100, j=0, sum=0;`
		` while (j < i)`
		` {`
		`sum = sum + i + j;`
		`i = i + 1;`

	`printf("%d, %d, %d",i, j, sum);`
	`}`
		`j = j + 2;`
		`}`
		`printf("%d, %d, %d",i,j,sum);}`

Program 4.1.4	`#include<stdio.h>`
	`void main()`
	`{`
	`int i,sum=0;`
	`for(i=0; ; i++)`
	`{`
	`sum = sum + i;`
	`printf("%d %d",i,sum);`
	`}`
	`}`
	
	`/*This is an infinite loop. */`
		`#include<stdio.h>`
		`void main()`
		`{`
		`int i,sum=0;`
		`i = 0;`
		`while(1)`
		`{`
		`sum = sum + i;`
		`printf("%d %d",i,sum);`
		`i++;`
		`}`
		`}`
		`/* This is an infinite loop. */`

Program 4.3 Write a program which prints positive integers from 1 to 300 with only three numbers in a line using *for* and *while* loop.

for loop

```
#include<stdio.h>
void main()
{
 int i;
 getchar();
          /* Enter <CR> for execution */
 for (i=1; i <=300; i = i+3)
     printf("%3d %3d %3d\n",i,i+1, i+2);
     getchar();
          /* Enter <CR> for termination */
 }
```

while loop

```
#include<stdio.h>
void main()
{
 int i = 1;
      while(i <= 300)
 {
 printf("%3d %3d %3d\n",i,i+1, i+2);
 i = i + 3;
 }
 getchar();
}
```

Output

```
1     2     3
4     5     6
7     8     9
10    11    12   and so on
```

Program 4.4 Write a program to sort integers from 1 through 500 into three groups, those divisible by 5 only, those divisible by 11 only and those divisible by 5 and 11. Find the total numbers in each group.

```
#include<stdio.h>
#include<math.h>
void main()
{
  int i, count5=0, count11=0, count511=0;
printf(“Press Enter Key <CR> \n”);
getchar();
for (i=1; i <= 500; i++)
    if((fmod(i,5) == 0) && (fmod(i,11) == 0))
    {
      count511++ ;
      printf(“%3d Divisible by 5 & 11.\n”,i);
    }
    else if(fmod(i,11) == 0)
    {
      count11++ ;
      printf(“\t %3d Divisible by 11.\n”,i);
    }
    else if(fmod(i,5) == 0)
    {
      count5++ ;
      printf(“\t\t %3d Divisible by 5.\n”, i);
    }
  printf(“Divisible by 5:%3d,”, count5);
  printf(“Divisible by 11:%3d,”, count11);
  printf(“Divisible by 5&11:%3d.\n”,count511);
  getchar();
}
```

/* i++ has the same meaning as i = i + 1

&& is the logical AND operator.

fmod function is available in math.h library file and hence included. sin, cos, exp, sqrt, etc. are also available in this library file. More details can be obtained from language reference manual / on line help. */

Output

```
Press Enter key <CR>
                    5 Divisible by 5.
                    10 Divisible by 5.
       11 Divisible by 11.
                    15 Divisible by 5.
                    20 Divisible by 5.
       22 Divisible by 11.
              .
              .
495 Divisible by 5 & 11.
Divisible by 5: 91, Divisible by 11: 36,
Divisible by 5 & 11: 9.
```

Program 4.5 An amount of Rs. 5000 is deposited in a SB account at 13% compound interest annually. Write a program to print the amount of account in each year for 20 years.

```
#include<stdio.h>
#define RATE 13.0
/* Note that there is no semi column at the end
of define statement. */
void main()
{
 int year;
 float principal=5000;
for(year = 1; year <=20; year++)
 {
     principal = principal * (1 +RATE/100);
     printf("Year:%2d,",year);
```

```
        printf("Amount:%6.0f\n", principal)
    }
    printf("Enter <CR> \n");
    getchar();
}
/* printf statements can be combined. */
```

Output

```
Year: 1, Amount: 5650
Year: 2, Amount: 6384
.
.
Year: 20, Amount: 57615
Enter <CR>
```

Program 4.6 Write a program to determine the number of years for exceeding Rs. 5000 for an initial deposit of Rs. 1000 at 13% compound interest annually.

```
#include<stdio.h>
void main()
{
  int year;
  float principal=1000, rate= 13;
  for(year = 1; principal <= 5000; year++)
      principal = principal * (1 + rate/100);
  printf("Year:%2d,",year);
  printf("Amount:%6.0f\n",principal);
  printf("Enter <CR> \n");
  getchar();
}
```

Output

```
Year: 15, Amount: 5535
Enter <CR>
```

Note: In program 4.6, the termination condition of *for* loop does not depends upon the value of the index year. The loop is terminated when *principal <=5000* becomes zero (false).

Program 4.7 Write a program which prints all odd positive numbers less than 100 omitting those divisible by 7.

```
#include<stdio.h>
#include<math.h>
void main()
{
  int i;
  for (i=1; i <100; i = i+2)
    if(fmod(i,7) != 0)
  printf("%3d,",i);
  printf("\nEnter <CR> \n");
  getchar();
}
```

Output

```
1, 3, 5, 9, 11, 13, ... and so on up to 99.
```

Program 4.8 z is a function of x, y and is given as

$$z = x^2 - 2xy + 3y^2 - 8x + 3y - 8$$

Write a program to calculate and print x, y and z when x and y both change from –3 to 3 with an increment of 0.2.

```
#include<stdio.h>
void main()
{
  double x,y,z;
  for(x = -3.0; x<= 3.0; x = x + 0.2)
  {
  for(y = -3.0; y <= 3; y = y + 0.2)
  {
   z = x*x - 2*x*y + 3 *y*y - 8 *x + 3*y - 8;
   printf("x=%4.1f, y=%4.1f, z=%6.2f\n",x,y,z);
  }
  printf("Press <CR> \n");
  getchar();
```

```
  }
}
```

Output

```
x = -3.0, y = -3.0, z = 25.00
x = -3.0, y = -2.8, z = 25.32
x = -3.0, y = -2.6, z = 21.88
.
.
Press <CR>
x = -2.8, y = -3.0, z = 23.44
x = -2.8, y = -2.8, z = 21.68
....... and so on
```

Program 4.9 Write a program for displaying a table of Fahrenheit and corresponding degree celsius. Use symbolic constants for upper and lower limits.

```
#include<stdio.h>
#define LOWER 0
#define UPPER 96
#define STEP 32
void main()
{
  int f; float deg;
  printf(" F C \n");
  printf(" ———— \n");
  for(f = LOWER; f <= UPPER; f=f + STEP)
  {
    deg = 5 * (f-32) / 9;
    printf("%3d %6.2f \n",f,deg);
  }
}
```

Output

```
 F        C
-------------
 0     -17.00
32       0.00
64      17.00
96      35.00
```

4.3 *do-while* Loop

If the *while* loop checks the condition at the beginning of the loop, *do-while* loop checks at the end. Hence, the body of the loop will be executed at least once. The syntax is given below.

do

statement$_1$

while(expression); ← **This loop will be executed at least once**

Program 4.10 Write a program which prints the positive integers from 1 to 300 with three numbers to a line only. Use *do-while* statement.

```
#include<stdio.h>
void main()
{
 int i=1;
 getchar();
 do
 {
     printf("%3d %3d %3d \n",i,i+1,i+2);
     i = i + 3;
 }
 while(i <= 300);
 getchar();
}
```

Output

```
1      2      3
4      5      6
7      8      9
10     11     12  and so on
```

4.4 *switch* Statement

switch statement is used for multi-way branching (decision-making) and can branch to a block (group of statements) for single value or multiple values of the expression. Sometimes *switch* statement is preferred over *if-else-if* ladder statement in C because of its simple and avoidance of confusion for multiple branching. Fig. 4.3 shows the flowchart of *switch* statement.

Syntax

```
switch (expression)
{
    case value1:
        statement1
        break;
    case value2:
        statement2
        break;
    ..........
    .........
    default:
        default block
        break;
}
statement-followed;
```

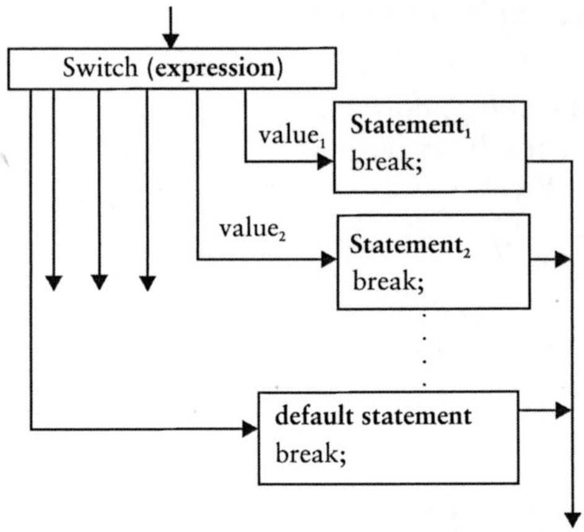

Fig. 4.3: Flowchart of *switch* statement

The expression is evaluated and the control is transferred to the corresponding *statement* (block). *Break* is used to terminate the *switch* block, after executing any one of the block. The *default* block will be executed if values of the expression do not match the value for any case. This statement is further explained with the following example.

Program 4.11 The category and the applicable sales tax percentage of different items in a super market are listed. Write a suitable program in C to find the selling price and sales tax of any given item. The total tax collected should be declared before terminating the program.

category	sales tax
1,2	10%
3	12%
4,8,10	13%
16,19	14%
others	5%

```
#include<stdio.h>
void main()
{
```

```
 int cat;
 float price = 0, salep = 0, tax = 0, totaltax = 0;
 printf("Enter the values of Category and Price.\n");
while(scanf("%d %f",&cat,&price) != EOF)
 {
   printf("Printed Price Rs %6.2f\n ",price);
 switch(cat)
 {
   case 1:
   case 2:
       tax = price * 0.1;
       break;
   case 3:
       tax = price * 0.12;
       break;
   case 4:
   case 8:
   case 10:
       tax = price * 0.13;
       break;
   case 16:
   case 19:
       tax = price * 0.14;
       break;
   default:
       tax = price * 0.05;
       break;
 }
 salep = price + tax;
 printf("\t\t\t Selling Price: Rs %6.2f \t(Tax: Rs
%5.2f)\n",salep,tax);
 totaltax = totaltax + tax;
 printf("Enter the values of Category and Price.\n");
 getchar();
 }
 printf("Total Tax collected %8.2f \n Good Bye !!
Enter <CR>",totaltax);
 getchar();
 }
```

Output

```
Enter the values of category and Price.
1 678 <CR>
Printed Price Rs 678.00
Selling Price:Rs 745.00  (Tax: Rs 67.80)
Enter the values of category and Price
16 200.5 <CR>
Printed Price Rs 200.50
Selling Price:Rs 228.57  (Tax:Rs 28.07)
5 300 <CR>
Printed Price Rs 300.00
Selling Price:Rs 315.00  (Tax:Rs 15.00)
^Z <CR>
Total Tax collected Rs 110.87
 Good Bye !! Enter <CR>
```

The *break* statement can be used in the body of *for, while*, and *do* for an early exit. The innermost enclosing loop will be exited.

Program 4.12 Illustration of break statement in *for* and *while* loop for conditional termination.

```
#include<stdio.h>
void main()
{
 int i, sum=0;
 for(i=0; ;i++)
 {
  sum = sum + i;
  if(sum > 1000)
  {
 printf("i = %d,
sum = %d\n",i,sum);
 break;

  }
 }
 printf("Outside the
loop.\n");
```

```
#include<stdio.h>
void main()
{
 int i,sum=0;
 i = 0;
 while(1)
 {
  sum = sum + i;
  i++;
       if(sum > 1000)
  {
 printf("i = %d, sum =
%d\n",i,sum);
  break;
  }
 }
  printf("Outside the
loop.\n");
```

```
  getchar();
}
/*This is not an
infinite loop. Refer
program 4.1.4 without
break statement.*/
```

```
  getchar();
}
/*This is not an infinite
loop. See program 4.1.4
with infinite while loop.*/
```

Output

```
i = 45, sum = 1035
Outside the loop.
```

4.5 *goto* Statement

Authors are not recommending for the use of unconditional *goto* for normal coding. It is easy to write readable codes without using it. However, this shall be useful in a deeply nested structure to abandon processing as follows.

```
for(......)
        for(.....)
        {
                ......
                if(disaster)
                  goto error;
        }
...........
error:
        (corrective/possible action)
```

The equivalent code for the following *goto* version program is given in program 4.1.1 (page 43) with an infinite *while* loop.

```
#include<stdio.h>
void main()
{
  float a,b,c,sum,avg;
  read:
  scanf("%f %f %f",&a, &b, &c);
  sum = a + b + c;
  avg = sum /3;
```

```
    printf("Sum = %6.2f, Average = %5.2f\n",sum,avg);
     goto read;
  }
```

The above program shall be terminated with a ^C !!.

The *goto* statements in C are **not used elsewhere in this text**, as it is rarely required and is unprofessional to use.

4.6 *continue* Statement

The **continue** statement in C programming language works somewhat like the **break** statement. Instead of forcing termination, however, continue forces the next iteration of the loop to take place, skipping any code in between.

For the **for** loop, **continue** statement causes the conditional test and increment portions of the loop to execute. For the **while** and **do...while** loops, **continue** statement causes the program control passes to the conditional tests.

Syntax:

The syntax for a **continue** statement in C is as follows:

```
continue;
```

Example:

```
for (int j=0; j<=8; j++)
{
  if (j==4)
  {
  continue;
  }
  printf("%d ", j);
}
```

Output:

```
0 1 2 3 5 6 7 8
```

4.7 Solved Programs

Program 4.13 A student has to get at least 50 or above marks in all three subjects for passing. FIRST CLASS and DISTINCTION are awarded for the passed students, according to their average marks. An average of 80% and above mark required for

DISTINCTION and 60% or above but below 80% mark is required for FIRST CLASS. The max mark in any subject is 100.

```
 /* Result declaration. */
#include<stdio.h>
#define TOTAL 20
void main()
{
 int mark1,mark2,mark3,average;
 int index;
 char *name[20]; /* array of 20 characters for
storing name. */
 for(index=1; index <= TOTAL; index++)
 {
 mark1=mark2=mark3=0;
 scanf(" %s %d %d %d",name,&mark1, &mark2, &mark3);
 if((mark1 > 100) || (mark2 > 100) || (mark3 >100))
   printf("Data Entry Error !!!!!.\n");
 else
   if((mark1 > 49) && (mark2 > 49) && (mark3 >
49))
   {
   average = (mark1 + mark2 + mark3) /3;
   printf("%20s %d ", name,average);
 if(average >79)
   printf(" DISTINCTION \n");
   else if (average >59)
   printf(" FIRST CLASS \n");
   else
   printf(" PASSED \n");
   }
   else
   printf("%s FAILED \n",name);
 }
}
```

/* TOTAL decides the sets of data (Now 20) to be entered. All data entry for marks above 100 is treated as ERROR. 'else if (average > 59)' control will be executed only if the average is less than or equal to 80. Data (John 59 60 60) does not declare a FIRST CLASS, i.e. rounding off is not possible and truncating the decimal part is done in integer mode. */

Output

```
John 59 99 87 <CR>
John 81 DISTINCTION
Ram 60 70 90 <CR>
Ram 73 FIRST CLASS
Ahmed 76 89 99 <CR>
Ahmed 88 DISTINCTION
Kennedy 41 99 56 <CR>
Kennedy FAILED
Mohasen 59 60 60 <CR>
Mohasen PASSED
....... and so on for 20 sets of Data.
```

Program 4.14 C program to print prime numbers between 1 and 100.

```
#include<stdio.h>
#include<math.h>
#include<conio.h>
void main()
{
  int i, j,flag;
  for(i=1; i<=100; i++)
  {flag=0;
  for(j=2; j<=sqrt(i); j++)
  {
  if(i%j==0)
  {
  flag=1;
  break;
  }
}
  if (flag==0)
  printf("%d\n",i);
  }
  getch();
}
```

```
1
2
3
5 and so on
```

Program 4.15 Write a program that accepts a number from 0 to 9 along with a string to be displayed a specified number of times. Use “switch-case” construct.

```
#include<stdio.h>
#include<conio.h>
void main()
{
int n,i;
char s[10];
clrscr();
printf("Enter a digit between 0 and 9: ");
scanf("%d",&n);
flushall();
printf("\nEnter the string to be displayed: ");
scanf("%s",s);
switch(n)
{case 0:   printf("ZERO");
           break;
case 1: for(i=0;i<n;i++)
           printf("\n%s",s);
           break;
case 2: for(i=0;i<n;i++)
           printf("\n%s",s);
           break;
case 3: for(i=0;i<n;i++)
           printf("\n%s",s);
           break;
case 4: for(i=0;i<n;i++)
           printf("\n%s",s);
           break;
```

```
case 5: for(i=0;i<n;i++)
            printf("\n%s",s);
            break;
case 6: for(i=0;i<n;i++)
            printf("\n%s",s);
            break;
case 7: for(i=0;i<n;i++)
            printf("\n%s",s);
            break;
case 8: for(i=0;i<n;i++)
            printf("\n%s",s);
            break;
case 9: for(i=0;i<n;i++)
            printf("\n%s",s);
            break;
default:printf("Invalid Digit");
}
getch();
}
```

Output

```
Enter a digit between 0 and 9:3
Enter the string to be displayed:apple
apple
apple
apple
```

Program 4.16 Program to find the Pythagorean triplets in the range 100 to 1000.

```
#include<stdio.h>
void main()
{
 int LegOne, LegTwo, Hypotenuse;
 Hypotenuse = 0;
 while ( Hypotenuse < 50 )
 {
 LegTwo = 1;
 while ( LegTwo < 50 )
 {
```

```
  LegOne = 1;
   while ( LegOne < 50 )
  {
   if ( LegOne*LegOne + LegTwo*LegTwo ==
Hypotenuse*Hypotenuse && LegOne < LegTwo )
  {
   printf("\n\t\t The sides are %4d,%4d,%4d",
LegOne,LegTwo,Hypotenuse);
  }
  LegOne++;
  }
  LegTwo++;
  }
  Hypotenuse++;
  }
printf("\n\n");
getch();
  }
```

Output

```
The sides are 8, 15, 17
The sides are 12, 16, 20
The sides are 15, 20, 25
The sides are 7, 24, 25
The sides are 10, 24, 26
The sides are 20, 21, 29
The sides are 18, 24, 30
The sides are 16, 30, 34
The sides are 21, 28, 35
The sides are 12, 35, 37
The sides are 15, 36, 39
The sides are 24, 32, 40
The sides are 9, 40, 41
The sides are 27, 36, 45 and so on
```

Program 4.17 Write a program to find the sum of the series x–x2/2! + x3/3! – x4/4! + x5/5! – x6/6!

```
#include<stdio.h>
#include<conio.h>
#include<math.h>
long int factorial(int n)
```

```
{
int i,f=1;
for(i=1;i<=n;i++)
f=f*i;
return(f);
}
void main()
{
int limit,x,j;
float sum=0.0;
long int k;
printf("Enter the Limit: ");
scanf("%d",&limit);
printf("\nEnter the value of x: ");
scanf("%d",&x);
for(j=0;j<limit;j++)
{
k=factorial(j+1);
sum+=pow(-1,j)*(pow(x,j+1)/k);
}
printf("Sum of the series = %f",sum);
getch();
}
```

Output

```
Enter the Limit:3
Enter the value of x:2
Sum of the series=1.33333
```

Program 4.18 Write a program to evaluate the function sin x = x – x3/3! + x5/5! – x7/7!.... to 0.0001 % accuracy.

```
#include<stdio.h>
#include<conio.h>
#include<math.h>
double fact(double power)
{
double f=1;
int k;
```

```
for(k=1;k<=power;k++)
f=f*k;
return f;
}
void main()
{
int i=1;
double x,term,deno,lob,sin,power=3;
clrscr();
printf("Enter the value for x: ");
scanf("%lf",&x);
term=x;
sin=x;
while(term>=0.0001)
{
lob=pow(x,power);
deno=fact(power);
term=lob/deno;
power+=2;
if(i%2==1)
sin=sin-term;
else
sin=sin+term;
i++;
}
printf("The result= %lf",sin);
getch();
}
```

Output

```
Enter the value for x:2
The result:0.909206
```

Program 4.19 Write a program to generate and print the first 10 members of the Fibonacci series.

```
/* Displaying Fibonacci sequence of first 10 terms */
#include<stdio.h>
 void main()
```

```
{
 int count, t1=0, t2=1, display=0;
    printf("Fibonacci Series of first 10 terms:
%d\n%d\n", t1, t2); /* Displaying first two terms */
 count=2; /* count=2 because first two terms are
already displayed. */
 while (count<10)
 {
 display=t1+t2;
 t1=t2;
 t2=display;
 ++count;
 printf("%d\n",display);
 }
 getch();
}
```

Output

```
Fibonacci Series of first 10 terms:
0
1
1
2
3
5
8
13
21
34
```

Program 4.20 Write a 'C' program to find the sum of the first 50 even numbers.

```
#include<stdio.h>
void main()
{int i,sum=0;
clrscr();
for(i=2;i<=100;i+=2)
sum=sum+i;
printf("Sum of first 50 even numbers=%d",sum);
```

```
getch();
}
```

Output

```
Sum of first 50 even numbers=2550
```

Program 4.21 Write an interactive C program to check whether the given number n is a prime. If not, find out and print any two factors of the given number n.

```
#include<stdio.h>
#include<math.h>
#include<conio.h>
void main()
{
  int n,j,flag,f1,f2;
  clrscr();
  printf("Enter a number: ");
scanf("%d",&n);
  flag=0;
  for(j=2; j<=n/2; j++)
  {
  if(j*j==n)/*perfect square number*/
{flag=1;
f1=j;
f2=j;
break;
}
  if((n%j==0)&&(flag==0))/*first factor*/
  {
  flag=1;
  f1=j;
  continue;
  }
if((n%j==0)&&(flag==1))/*second factor*/
{
```

```
flag=2;
f2=j;
break;
}
} if (flag==0)
 printf(“The number %d is prime\n”,n);
 else
 {printf(“The number %d is not prime\n”,n);
printf(“The two factors of %d is %d and %d”,n,f1,f2);
}
 getch();
}
```

Output

```
Enter a number:6
The number 6 is not prime
The two factors of 6 is 2 and 3
```

Program 4.22 Evaluate sin(x) for x in the range 0 to 900 at intervals of 50 and print the result as a table. Use trapezoidal rule.

```
#include<stdio.h>
#include<math.h>
void main(){
int i;
float result;
for(i=0;i<90;i=i+5){
/*Interval is 5 and hence 2.5 is half the interval*/
result=2.5*(sin(i)+sin(i+5));
printf(“\nIntegral %d to %d= %f\n”,i,i+5,result);
}
getch();
}
```

Output

```
Integral 0 to 5   = -2.397311
Integral 5 to 10  = -3.757364
Integral 10 to 15 = 0.265667 and so on
```

Program 4.23 Write a C program to evaluate e^x to an accuracy of 10^{-5}.

```
#include<stdio.h>
#include<conio.h>
void main()
{
  int i, n, exp;
  float x, sum = 1, t = 1 ;
  clrscr() ;
  printf("Enter the value for x : ") ;
  scanf("%f", &x) ;
  printf("\nEnter the value for n : ") ;
  scanf("%d", &n) ;
  for(i = 1 ; i < n + 1 ; i++)
  {
      exp = i ;
      t = t * x / exp;
      sum = sum + t;
  }
  printf("\nExponential Value of %f is : %8.5f",
x, sum) ;
  getch() ;
}
```

Output

```
Enter the value for x : 3
Enter the value for n : 4
Exponential value of 3.000000 is : 16.37500
```

Exercise for Computer Lab

Exercise E4.1 Team A and B are playing game X. Whoever is making the first 50 points or more will be declared as the winner. Write a C program to chose the winner. Both teams may get 1 to 5 points in each game.

Exercise E4.2 Write a C program to display a timer on the screen with the format (hh:mm:ss) and verify the result.

Exercise E4.3 Team A and B are playing basketball. Show their score board with a timer. Remember the timeout should not be counted by the timer and the score is given through the keyboard. Display the number of timeouts by each team on the screen.

Exercise E4.4 A tax collecting center is collecting tax for five regions. Each remitter has a unique five digit ID number. Write a C program to report the total collection from each region and the grand total of daily collection.

4.8 Summary

We learned to transfer the sequence of program execution using branching, looping and jumping control statements in C. It is required for conditional branching, repeating the loop for finite and infinite number of times. We shall study the details of arrays and strings in next chapter to follow.

4.9 Review Questions

1. Which are conditional and branching statements?
2. Explain looping statements with examples.
3. What is the use of jumping statements? Give examples.
4. Where do you use *break* statement?
5. What are the uses of a jumping statement? Give examples.
6. Differentiate break and continue.
7. Give an example for exit controlled loop and explain.
8. Explain the use of break and switch with the help of example.
9. How does switch statement differ from nested if?

10. What is a nested loop?
11. Give the syntax for 'do-while' statement. Give an example.
12. Explain nested for loop with suitable example.
13. Explain the difference between 'while' and 'do-while' with an example program.
14. What is the purpose of the index in a for statement?

CHAPTER 5 Arrays

5.1 Introduction

An array is a data type which is used to group homogeneous data item named under a common subscripted variable name. The homogeneous nature of these data items and its reference with an index makes the programming much easier and efficient. C allows three or more dimensional arrays and the exact dimension is implementation dependent.

5.2 One Dimensional Array (Single Dimensional Array)

Many a times we need to manipulate homogeneous data in our daily applications. For an example, if we need to record the *rollno* of students in a class. Assuming *rollno* are of *integer* type, one and only way to manipulate these data, by considering the methods what we have studied so far, has to declare as many *integer* variable as the number of students like

```
int rollno_1,rollno_2,......,rollno_n;
```

This is practical if we have only few students in the class, and is very difficult to handle these declared variables if the *n* is large. The solution is to use one dimensional array. By using array we can handle this large data by a single variable name with an index giving each rollno(s).

The general form for declaring one dimensional array is

type variable_name[size];

As any other variable, all arrays shall be explicitly declared in C in order to allocate space in the memory. The total size allocated will be depending on the *type* and the *size* specified in the declaration statement. For example, if *type* is *int* and *size* is *10*, the total space allocated will be 20 bytes, assuming *int* takes 2 bytes of memory space.

So for our example of recording student's rollno, we need to declare it like this

```
int rollno[100];
```

if total number of students is *100*, assuming *rollno* consist only integer numbers. That is, the above statement declares that the *rollno* is an array variable that will contain only *integer* type values and has a total of *100* elements. It should be noted that in C, array indexing always starts at 0.

5.3 Initialization of Arrays

Arrays can be initialized like any other variables by following its declaration with a list of initializers enclosed in braces and separated by commas. The general form of initialization of arrays is,

type variable_name[size] = {list of values};

For example,

```
int rollno[3] = {10,11,12};
```

When the size of an array is omitted, the size will be taken by length of initializers. For example,

```
int rollno[] = {10,11,12};
```

Note: If there are fewer intializers for an array than the size specified, the missing elements will taken as zero. It is an error to have too many intializers.

5.3.1 Character Array

Character array may have special intilization syntax. Here a string may be used instead of braces and commas notation. For example,

```
char name[] = "John";
```

is a shorthand for longer but equivalent

```
char name[] = {'J','o','h','n'};
```

5.4 Multidimensional Array

Having studied the declaration of one dimensional array, the idea of declaring multidimensional array is also simple in C language. With two bracket pairs, we obtain a two-dimensional array and by adding more bracket pairs, we obtain higher dimensional arrays.

5.4.1 Two Dimensional Array

The general form of two-dimensional array declaration is

type variable_name[size][size];

We can explain the concept of Two-dimensional array by extending our previous example. Now consider we need to record five marks each of three students having their corresponding rollno. We will have a declaration like this

```
int mark[3][5];
```

Here, 3 represent the number of students/rollno and 5 represent the corresponding five marks of each student. Even though array elements are stored contiguously in memory, it is convenient to think two-dimensional array as a rectangular collection of elements with rows and columns. A diagrammatic representation of the above representation will be

	Mark_1	Mark_2	Mark_3	Mark_4	Mark_5
Rollno_1	mark[0][0]	mark[0][1]	mark[0][2]	mark[0][3]	mark[0][4]
Rollno_2	mark[1][0]	mark[1][1]	mark[1][2]	mark[1][3]	mark[1][4]
Rollno_3	mark[2][0]	mark[2][1]	mark[2][2]	mark[2][3]	mark[2][4]

The following program illustrates the initialization of single and two dimensional arrays.

Program 5.1 Illustration of one/two dimensional array declaration and initialization.

```
#include<stdio.h>
void main()
{
     static int x[3] = {1,1,1};
     static int z[] = {1,1,1,1};
     static int y[2][4] = {1,1,1,1,0,0,0,0};
     static int a[2][4] = {{1},
                           {0,1}};
     int i,j;
     for (i=0; i<3 ; i++)
     printf(“x[%1d] = %1d ”,i,x[i]);
     printf(“\n”);
     for (i=0; i<3 ; i++)
     printf(“z[%1d] = %1d ”,i,z[i]);
     printf(“\n\n”);
     for (i=0 ; i < 2 ; i++)
     {
           for(j=0; j < 4 ; j++)
           printf(“y[%1d][%1d] = %1d ”,i,j,y[i][j]);
           printf(“\n”);
     }
     printf(“\n”);
     for (i=0 ; i < 2 ; i++)
     {
     for(j=0; j < 4 ; j++)
           printf(“a[%1d][%1d] = %1d ”,i,j,a[i][j]);
           printf(“\n”);
     }
           getchar();
}
```

Output

```
x[0] = 1 x[1] = 1 x[2] = 1
z[0] = 1 z[1] = 1 z[2] = 1
y[0][0] = 1 y[0][1] = 1 y[0][2] = 1 y[0][3] = 1
y[1][0] = 0 y[1][1] = 0 y[1][2] = 0 y[1][3] = 1
a[0][0] = 1 a[0][1] = 0 a[0][2] = 0 a[0][3] = 0
a[1][0] = 0 a[1][1] = 1 a[1][2] = 0 a[1][3] = 0
```

More programs of the above type shall be done to familiar with the subscripts and value storing and retrieval mechanism in an array.

5.5 One Dimensional Array—Solved Sample Programs

Program 5.2 Write a C program for counting the numbers greater than 50 for 20 data input.

```
#include<stdio.h>
void main()
{
  int b[19];
  int i, count=0;
  printf(“Input 20 data. \n”);
/* reading data and storing to an array */
  for (i=0; i < 20; i++)
    scanf(“%d”, &b[i]);
  /* retrieving all the elements of the array,
printing the values greater than 50, and
      incrementing the counter */
  for (i=0; i < 20 ; i++)
    if(b[i] > 50)
    {
      printf(“%d\t”,b[i]);
      count = count + 1;
    }
  printf(“\n%d numbers are greater than 50.\n”,count);
  getchar();
}
```

Output

```
Input data. Message
20 30 56 67 65 34 34 2 3 5 98 896
457 789 6 54 45 23 76 568 <CR>
10 numbers are greater than 50.
```

Bubble sort

Given a list of unsorted integers. Sort the elements of the list in ascending order.

Approach

Compare the first element of the list (i^{th} element) with the remaining n-1 elements (j^{th} element), i.e. 1st element with 2nd, 3rd, 4th and so on till the last element. The process is repeated with comparison of ith and j^{th} elements and the smallest element is kept in i^{th} position for ascending order. For descending order biggest element is kept in i^{th} position.

The loop will be repeated with 2nd element with the 3rd, 4th, 5th and so on till the last element and the smallest element is kept in i^{th} location.

The steps are repeated till the $(n-1)^{th}$ element compares with n^{th} element.

This sorting method is called **bubble sort.**

Program 5.3 Write a C program for reading a list of integers and sort the numbers in ascending order using bubble sort algorithm. The list may contain maximum of 100 elements.

```
#include<stdio.h>
#define MAXSIZE 100
void main()
{
  int list[MAXSIZE],temp,i=0,j=0,size=0;
  printf("Enter data, terminate by F6 or ^Z <CR>\n");
  while(scanf("%d",&list[i]) != EOF)
    i++;
  size = i;
  for(i= 0; i < (size-1); i++)
  for(j = i+1; j< size; j++)
    if(list[i] > list[j])
    {
            /* swapping the elements , keeping the
smallest element in list[i] */
      temp = list[i];
      list[i] = list[j];
      list[j] = temp;
    }
```

swapping the elements of ith and j^{th} location

```
  printf("Sorted list is\n");
  for(i=0; i < size ; i++)
    printf("%d\t",list[i]);
  getchar();
}
```

Output

```
Enter data, terminated by F6 or ^Z <CR>
14 32 84 232 10 8 4 <CR> F6 <CR>
Sorted list is
4 8 10 14 32 84 232
```

Program 5.4 Write a program to accept a list of integers (Max = 100 elements) and print each pair of integers whose sum is 100, each pair on a separate line.

```
#include<stdio.h>
#define MAXSIZE 100
void main()
{
  int list[MAXSIZE],i=0,j,size;
  printf("Enter data, terminate by F6 or ^Z <CR>\n");
  while(scanf("%d",&list[i]) != EOF)
    i++;
  size = i;
  for(i= 0; i < (size-2); i++)
  for(j = i+1; j < size; j++)
    if((list[i] + list[j])== 100)
    printf("%d %d \n",list[i],list[j]);
    getchar();
}
```

Output

```
Enter data, terminate by F6 or ^Z <CR>
1 3 4 2 34 97 23 99 42 96 23 3 77
<CR> ^Z <CR>
3 97
4 96
97 3
23 77
23 77
```

5.6 Two Dimensional Arrays—Solved Sample Programs

Program 5.5 Write a C program to find the sum of two matrix of order L x M.

```
#include<stdio.h>
#include<conio.h>
void main()
{
  int a[10][10], b[10][10], c[10][10];
  int m,n,row,col;
  printf("Input No. of rows & No. of columns.\n");
  scanf("%d %d",&m, &n);
 printf("Input the data row by row for Matrix A\n");
/* reading first matrix */
  for(row = 0; row < m; row++)
  for(col = 0; col < n; col++)
    scanf("%d",&a[row][col]);
  printf("\nInput the data row by row for Matrix
B\n");
/* reading second matrix */
  for(row = 0; row < m; row++)
  for(col = 0; col < n; col++)
    scanf("%d",&b[row][col]);
  /* Addition of two matrix. */
  for(row = 0; row < m; row++)
  for(col = 0; col < n; col++)
    c[row][col] = a[row][col] + b[row][col] ;
  printf("\nThe sum of matrix A and B is \n");
/* printing the matrix c, row by row */
  for(row = 0; row < m; row++)
  {
  for(col = 0; col < n; col++)
  printf("%d\t",c[row][col]);
  printf("\n");
  }
  getchar(); getchar();
}
```

Output

```
Input No. of rows & No. of columns.
2 2 <CR>
Input the data row by row for Matrix A.
4 2 <CR>
6 8 <CR>
Input the data row by row for Matrix B.
8 3 <CR>
5 7 <CR>
The sum of Matrix A and B is
12 5
11 15
<CR>
```

Program 5.6 Write a C program to multiply a matrix of any order.

```
#include<stdio.h>
#include<conio.h>
void main()
{
  int a[10][10], b[10][10], c[10][10];
  int i,k,j,row,col,indx;
  printf(“Input the values I,K,J for two matrix A(I,K), B(K,J)\n”);
  scanf(“%d %d %d”,&i, &k, &j);
  printf(“Input the data row by row for Matrix A.\n”);
/* reading matrix a */
  for(row = 0; row < i; row++)
  for(col = 0; col < k; col++)
    scanf(“%d”,&a[row][col]);
  printf(“Input the data row by row for Matrix B.\n”);
/* reading matrix b */
  for(row = 0; row < k; row++)
  for(col = 0; col < j ; col++)
    scanf(“%d”,&b[row][col]);
  /* Multiplication of two matrix, and store the result in matrix c. */
```

← The maximum size of array can be increased later, if required. Or use *#define* statement.

```
  for(row = 0; row < i; row++)
  for(col = 0; col < j ; col++)
  {
    c[row][col] = 0;
    for(indx = 0; indx < k; indx++)
   c[row][col] = c[row][col] + a[row][indx] * b[indx]
[col] ;
  }
  printf("The Product of matrix A and B is \n");
  for(row = 0; row < i; row++)
  {
  for(col = 0; col < j; col++)
    printf("%d\t",c[row][col]);
  printf("\n");
  }
  getchar(); getchar();
}
```

Output

```
Input the values I,K,J for two
A(I,K), B(K,J)
3 2 4 <CR>
Input the data row by row for matrix A.
1 2 <CR>
3 4 <CR>
5 6 <CR>
Input the data row by row for matrix B.
9 8 7 6 <CR>
5 4 3 2 <CR>
The product of matrix A and B is
19 16 13 10
47 40 33 26
75 64 53 42
<CR>
```

Program 5.7 Write a C program to rearrange the elements of each row of the following matrix such that the elements of each row of the matrix are arranged in descending order.

```
#include<stdio.h>
#include<conio.h>
```

```
void main()
{
  int a[10][10],tmp;
  int i,j,row,col,indx;
   printf("Input the values I and J of matrix
A(I,J)\n");
  scanf("%d %d",&i,&j);
  printf("Input the data row by row for Matrix
A.\n");
  for(row = 0; row < i; row++)
  for(col = 0; col < j; col++)
    scanf("%d",&a[row][col]);

  /* Sorting each row of a matrix. */
  for(row = 0; row < i; row++)
  for(col = 0; col < (j-1) ; col++)
    for(indx = col+1; indx < j; indx++)
      if(a[row][col] < a[row][indx])
      {
        tmp = a[row][col];
        a[row][col] = a[row][indx];
        a[row][indx] = tmp;
      }
  printf("The sorted matrix.\n");
  for(row = 0; row < i; row++)
  {
  for(col = 0; col < j; col++)
    printf("%d\t",a[row][col]);
  printf("\n");
  }
  getchar(); getchar();
}
```

Output

```
Input the values I
and J of matrix A(I,J)
4 4 <CR>
Input the data row by
row for matrix A.
-10 9 8 15 <CR>
3 12 2 -4 <CR>
6 8 3 1 <CR>
1 -5 9 -3 <CR>
```

```
The sorted matrix.
15 9 8 -10
12 3 2 -4
8 6 3 1
9 1 -3 -5
<CR>
```

5.7 Solved Programs

Program 5.8 A and B are two given one-dimensional arrays. Read them and sort them in ascending order. Then merge them into a single sorted array C in the ascending order.

```
#include<stdio.h>
 void merge(int [], int, int [], int, int []);
 void main() {
 int a[100], b[100], m, n, c,d,t,sorted[200];
  printf("Input number of elements in first array\n");
   scanf("%d", &m);
   printf("Input %d integers\n", m);
   for (c = 0; c < m; c++) {
   scanf("%d", &a[c]);
   }
   for(c=0;c<m-1;c++){
   for(d=c+1;d<m;d++)
   if(a[c]>a[d]){
   t=a[c];
   a[c]=a[d];
   a[d]=t;
   }
   }
  printf("Input number of elements in second
array\n");
   scanf("%d", &n);
   printf("Input %d integers\n", n);
   for (c = 0; c < n; c++) {
   scanf("%d", &b[c]);
   }
   for(c=0;c<m-1;c++){
   for(d=c+1;d<m;d++)
   if(b[c]>b[d]){
   t=b[c];
   b[c]=b[d];
   b[d]=t;
   }
```

```
    }
    merge(a, m, b, n, sorted);
    printf("Sorted array:\n");
    for (c = 0; c < m + n; c++) {
    printf("%d\n", sorted[c]);
  }
    getch();
}
void merge(int a[], int m, int b[], int n, int
sorted[]) {
    int i, j, k;
    j = k = 0;
    for (i = 0; i < m + n;) {
    if (j < m && k < n) {
    if (a[j] < b[k]) {
       sorted[i] = a[j];
       j++;
    }
    else {
       sorted[i] = b[k];
         k++;
       }
       i++;
  }
  else if (j == m) {
    for (; i < m + n;) {
       sorted[i] = b[k];
       k++;
       i++;
    }
  }
  else {
    for (; i < m + n;) {
       sorted[i] = a[j];
       j++;
       i++;
       }
      }
    }
}
```

Output

```
Input number of elements in first array
3
Input 3 integers
4
5
3
Input number of elements in second array
2
Input 2 integers
9
8
Sorted array:
3
4
5
8
9
```

Program 5.9 Write a program to find whether the matrix is symmetrical or not.

```
#include<stdio.h>
void main()
{
int n,i,j,flag=0;
int a[20][20];
printf("\nEnter the order of the Matrix: ");
scanf("%d",&n);
printf("\nEnter the matrix elements:");
for(i=0;i<n;i++)
for(j=0;j<n;j++)
scanf("%d",&a[i][j]);
for(i=0;i<n;i++)
{
for(j=0;j<n;j++)
{
if(a[i][j]!=a[j][i])
{
flag=1;
break;
}
```

```
}
if(flag==1) break;
}
printf(“Matrix\n”);
for(i=0;i<n;i++)
{
for(j=0;j<n;j++)
printf(“%d ”,a[i][j]);
printf(“\n”);
}
if(flag==1)
printf(“\n The Matrix is not Symmetric”);
else
printf(“\n The Matrix is Symmetric”);
getch();
}
```

Output

```
Enter the order of the Matrix:3
Enter the matrix elements:1 2 3 4 5 6 7 8 9
The Matrix is not Symmetric
```

Program 5.10 Write a program to find the largest element in an array and position of its occurence.

```
#include<stdio.h>
 void main() {
 int a[30], i, num, largest,pos;
 printf(“\nEnter no of elements :”);
 scanf(“%d”, &num);
 printf(“\nEnter the elements\n”);
 //Read n elements in an array
 for (i = 0; i < num; i++)
 scanf(“%d”, &a[i]);
 //Consider first element as largest
 largest = a[0];
 for (i = 0; i < num; i++) {
 if (a[i] > largest) {
 largest = a[i];
 pos=i;
```

```
  }
  }
  // Print out the Result
  printf(“\nLargest Element : %d at location %d”,
largest,pos);
   getch();
}
```

Output

```
Enter no of elements: 5
Enter the elements: 2 4 10 3 9
Largest Element: 10 at location 2
```

Program 5.11 Write a C Program to multiply a 3 x 5 array by a scalar.

```
#include<stdio.h>
void main()
{
int i,j,k;
int a[3][5];
printf(“\nEnter the matrix elements of a 3 X 5
Matrix:\n”);
for(i=0;i<3;i++)
for(j=0;j<5;j++)
scanf(“%d”,&a[i][j]);
printf(“\nEnter the scalar:”);
scanf(“%d”,&k);
for(i=0;i<3;i++){
for(j=0;j<5;j++)
{
a[i][j]=k*a[i][j];
}
}
printf(“Matrix\n”);
for(i=0;i<3;i++)
{
for(j=0;j<5;j++)
printf(“%d ”,a[i][j]);
printf(“\n”);
```

```
}
getch();
}
```

```
Enter the matrix elements of a 3 X 5
Matrix:
1 2 3 4 5 6 7 8 9 1 2 3 4 5 6
Enter the scalar:2
Matrix
2 4 6 8 10
12 14 16 18 2
4 6 8 10 12
```

5.8 Exercise for Computer Lab

Exercise E5.1 Write a C program to find the transpose of a matrix A.
Hint: b(i, j) = a(j, i), replace this logic in the above program 15.5 instead of addition.

Exercise E5.2 Write a C program to find the biggest element in each row of matrix of order (IxJ) and store the results in the (I, J+1)th location of the same matrix.

Exercise E5.3 Write a program for printing a sorted list of numbers above 50, using arrays. The program should accept data input from the keyboard until the user press F6.

Exercise E5.4 Write a C program to find the row and column total of a matrix of order (IxJ), and store the results in the (I, J+1)th location and (I+1, J)th locations. Verify the result such that the grand column total is equal to grand row total and the grand total should be available in (I+1, J+1)th location.

Exercise E5.5 Finding Saddle Point: If an element is minimum in one row and the same element is maximum in the column, then it is called a saddle point. Write a C program to find saddle points, if any, in a given matrix.

5.9 Summary

We have seen how to declare and initialize an array. Different retrieval mechanisms of one dimensional and two dimensional arrays using their subscripts were also discussed. We also have seen some simple programs in C using arrays.

5.10 Review Questions

1. What do you mean by subscripted variable?
2. What are the uses of subscripted variable and discuss the advantages over scalar variables?
3. How do you represent two dimensional arrays in C? Give examples.
4. What are the disadvantages of static arrays?
5. How do you initialize one dimensional and two dimensional arrays?

CHAPTER 6 Functions

6.1 Introduction

Functions in a program are used to perform certain tasks. In other perspective, function can be viewed as a sub-program, which contains group of statements that can be used repetitively in the main program. The advantage of a function is that, we can name this group of statements to use further in the main program. By giving a function name, we can call (invoke) functions by mentioning its name to perform the desired task. Usually, a function will contain those statements that are related to the desired task that it performs. One such function that every C program must have is the *main* function.

Any number of functions can be defined in a C program. Any two function definition cannot have the same name in a program. A function may take any number of input values called *arguments* and after performing the tasks, it might give back the result called *return value*. These functions, known as *user defined functions*, to differentiate from the library function in C like *printf* function.

<mention about *caller* and *callee*>

An example of one such user defined function is a function for adding two integer numbers. In this case, the function name can be *add*, the input values are two integer numbers, its task is to add the numbers and its return value is the sum of the two numbers.

So, the purpose of the function is to divide the main program into many subprograms and each subprogram performs certain task. This is similar to assignment of different jobs to different persons in a project. Each one will handle the assigned task and reports to the Manager. The Manager co-ordinates and control all activities.

6.2 Steps Involved in Writing a Function

6.2.1 Function Definition (Syntax)

Each function definition has the form

```
return_type function_name (argument_list)
{
        declaration and statements
        return ()
}
```

Every function definition comprises of two parts. First part is function *header*, i.e., the line before the first brace and everything inside the braces are the function *body*.

Function *header* again consists of three parts. First part is the *return_type*, i.e. the type of the value that the function returns. The type can be any data type that we have studied including *void*. If we mention *return_type* as *void*, this means that the function is not returning any value. If the *return_type* is omitted, it will automatically assume to be of the type *int*.

Second part is the *function_name*, the name by which the function is known. It must be unique in a program.

Third part is the *argument_list*. This the way by which a function will accept the values from outside. *Argument_list* is a list of *variables* and each *variable* must be separated by comma.

Among the three, various parts may be omitted; a minimal function is

dummy()

{}

which does nothing and return nothing.

Function body consists of variable declaration and statements that are used to perform the desired task. At the end the function will return value(s) using *return* statement.

The *return* statement is the mechanism for returning a value from the called function to its caller. The general form of *return* statement is as follows:

return(expression)

By giving this statement, the value of the *expression* will be returned by the function. Furthermore, a *return* statement terminates the function and passes the control back to the calling environment. Here it should be noted that the type of the value that is returned by a function should match with type given in the *reurn_type*. Parenthesis is often used around the *expression*, but they are optional.

Note: The calling function is free to ignore the values returned from the called function. Also, *expression* is optional in the *return* statement.

Note: A function can return only one value.

6.2.2 Function Prototype/Function Declaration

It is a good programming practice to declare all functions, before invoking them. The declaration statement of a function is known as "Function Prototype". It describes the function interface to the compiler by (optionally) giving details such as the number, type of arguments, and type of return value.

For an example, if we take a sum function which we described above the *Function Prototype* will be

int sum (int,int)

or

int sum (int x,int y).

From the above, one thing that should be noted that, the *argument/parameter name* are optional in the *Function Prototype*. This tells to compiler that *sum()* is a function that takes two arguments of type *int* and returns a *int.*

6.2.3 Function Call

Any function can be invoked using its name. Care should be taken to match the number of parameter and the parameter type. The given parameters while calling a function are called the *actual parameters* and the parameters in the function definition that receives the arguments are called *formal parameters*. For an example, calling the function *sum* should be like this:

sum(10, 20);

Here, the *sum* is the function name and *10* and *20* are its parameters.

6.2.4 Complete Program Using Function

```
int sum(int,int);              ←Function Prototype
void main()
{
  int result;
  result = sum(10,20);         ←Function Calling
  printf ("Result is %d", result);
}
int sum(int x, int y)          ←Function Definition
{
return (x+y);
}
```

6.3 Scope Rules

A scope in any programming is a region of the program where a defined variable can have its existence and beyond that variable it cannot be accessed. There are three places where variables can be declared in C programming language.

- Inside a function or a block which is called local variables.
- Outside of all functions which is called global variables.
- In the definition of function parameters which are called formal parameters.

6.3.1 Local Variables

Variables that are declared inside a function or block are called local variables. They can be used only by statements that are inside that function or block of code. Local variables are not known to functions outside their own. The following example shows how local variables are used. Here all the variables a, b, and c are local to main() function.

```
#include<stdio.h>
 void main() {
 /* local variable declaration */
 int a, b;
 int c;
 /* actual initialization */
 a = 10;
 b = 20;
 c = a + b;
printf ("value of a = %d, b = %d and c =
%d\n", a, b, c);
}
```

6.3.2 Global Variables

Global variables are defined outside a function, usually on top of the program. Global variables hold their values throughout the lifetime of your program and they can be accessed inside any of the functions defined for the program. A global variable can be accessed by any function. That is, a global variable is available for use throughout your entire program after its declaration. The following program show how global variables are used in a program.

```
#include<stdio.h>
  /* global variable declaration */
int g;
  void main() {
  /* local variable declaration */
  int a, b;
  /* actual initialization */
  a = 10;
  b = 20;
  g = a + b;
  printf ("value of a = %d, b = %d and g =
%d\n", a, b, g);
  }
```

A program can have same name for local and global variables but the value of local variable inside a function will take preference.

```
#include<stdio.h>
  /* global variable declaration */
  int g = 20;
  void main() {
  /* local variable declaration */
  int g = 10;
  printf ("value of g = %d\n", g);
  }
```

This will produce the result value of g = 10.

6.3.3 Formal Parameters

Formal parameters, are treated as local variables with-in a function and they take precedence over global variables. The following shows an example for formal parameters.

```
#include<stdio.h>
  /* global variable declaration */
int a = 20;
  void main() {
  /* local variable declaration in main function
*/
```

```
    int a = 10;
    int b = 20;
    int c = 0;
    printf ("value of a in main() = %d\n", a);
    c = sum(a, b);
    printf ("value of c in main() = %d\n", c);
    }
/* function to add two integers */
int sum(int a, int b) {
    printf ("value of a in sum() = %d\n", a);
    printf ("value of b in sum() = %d\n", b);
    return a + b;
}
```

When the above program is executed, it produce the following result.

```
value of a in main() = 10
value of a in sum() = 10
value of b in sum() = 20
value of c in main() = 30
```

6.4 Different Mechanisms in Function Calls

1. Call by value
2. Call by reference
3. Return by reference

6.4.1 Call by Value

The values of actual parameters are copied into formal parameters. The function cannot manipulate the actual parameter, but it can only modify the value of formal parameter.

```
void swap(int x, int y)
{
    int temp;
    temp = x;
    x = y;
    y = temp;
    printf("%d %d within swap function \n", x,y);
}
```

```
void main()
{
  int a=5, b=10;
  swap(a,b);
/* swapping does not take place. Refer call by
reference for swapping */
  printf("%d %d :After swapping \n", a,b);
}
```

To understand the mechanism of call by reference, we need to understand more about reference variable.

6.4.2 Reference Variable

A reference variable is an alias name for a previously defined variable. Both variables refer to the same address location. Hence, the change in value of any variable will reflects on the other variable. Only a reference is passed to the function. Reference variable is represented by using the Operator &.

6.4.3 Call by Reference

A reference to the actual variable (alias) is passed to the function. The formal parameters become references for the actual parameters. Hence, the function manipulates the actual data directly by fetching the same memory location. The changes made in the formal parameter will be reflected on the actual parameter also.

```
Eg:
void main()
{ int a,b;
  a=5; b=10;
  void swap(int &, int &)
  swap(a,b);
  printf("%d %d \n", a,b);
          getch();
}
void swap(int &x, int &y)
{
  int temp;
  temp = x;
```

```
    x = y;
    y = temp;
  }
```

6.4.4 Calling Function with Arrays

Only the address of the array needs to be passed, when an array is used as an argument to a function. The address of the array is the array name itself.

```
void main()
{
  int mark[50];
/* enter elements of array mark */
display(mark);
getch();
  }
  void display(int m[50])
  {
          for i=1,50
                  printf("%d \t", m[i]);
  }
```

6.4.5 Return by Reference

A function can return a reference variable. But a function returning a reference can appear LHS of an assignment statement.

```
float &min(float &a, float &b)
{
  If (a>b)
          return (a);
          /* returns the address of b */
  else
          return (b);
          /* returns the address of b */
}
```

6.5 Recursion

A function calling itself is called recursion. It can be represented in mathematics as n! = n (n-1)!

= n (n-1) (n-2)!

for example 4! = 4 * 3!

= 4 * 3 * 2!

= 4 * 3 * 2 * 1!

= 4 * 3 * 2 * 1 * 0!

= 4 * 3 * 2 * 1 * 1 = 24

Therefore the multiplication can be terminated when 0! is reached. This is illustrated in C function as shown below in the program 6.1.

Program 6.1 Illustration of n! using recursive function.

```
#include<stdio.h>
int factorial(int n);
void main()
{
  int n;
  printf("Enter a positive integer: ");
  scanf("%d",&n);
  printf("Factorial of %d = %d", n, factorial(n));
  }
int factorial(int n)
{
  if(n!=1)
  return n*factorial(n-1);
else
return 1;
}
```

Output

```
Enter a positive integer: 3
Factorial of 3=6
```

Sum of an array of integers can be written in mathematics as follows

S list(i) = list(n) + S list(i)

= list(n) + list(n-1) + S list(i)

= ....

= .... + list(0)

The above equation can represented in C by using recursion as shown in the program 6.13.

6.6 Solved Programs

Program 6.2 Function divisible to find out the given number is divisible by another number.

```
int divisible(num,divd)
int num,divd;
{
  if(num == 0)
  return 0;
  if(num/divd*divd == num)
  return divd;
  else
  return 0;
}
/* This function shall be included /added with any
other main application program. */
```

The above function checks the given number is divisible by another number. If it is divisible, returns the dividend (non zero, indicating true) otherwise returns zero (false). When the number is zero the function returns zero (false). The following main program along with the function *divisible* shows the top-down modular programming approach in a simple way.

Program 6.3 Main program & function *divisible* to find out the given number is divisible by another number.

```
/* Program for finding the given number is divisible
by another
  number using function subprogram */
#include<stdio.h>
int divisible();
void main()
{
  int number,divident;
  scanf("%d %d",&number,&divident);
```

← Function declaration
Note: int divisible(int, int); is also a valid prototype

```
  if(divisible(number,divident))
 printf("%d is divisible by %d.\n", number,divident);
  else
   printf("%d is not divisible by %d.\n",
number,divident);
   getchar();
}
int divisible(num,divd)
int num,divd;
{
  if(num == 0)
  return 0;
  if(num/divd*divd == num)
  return divd;
  else
  return 0;
}
```

Declaring the *type* of arguments

Output

```
39 13 <CR>
39 is divisible by 13
run
12 5 <CR>
12 is not divisible by 5
```

The function *divisible* is called from the main program and the logic becomes simple and readable.

Program 6.4 Write a C program for checking the given number is prime or not by using function.

```
/* Program to check the given number is prime or
not, using function */
#include<stdio.h>
int prime();
int divisible();
void main()
{
  int n;
  scanf("%d", &n);
  if(prime(n))
```

```
  printf("%d is prime.\n",n);
  else
  printf("%d is not prime.\n",n);
  getchar();
}
/* Function 'prime'. */
int prime(num)
int num;
{
  int k;
  if(num < 4)
  return 1;
  else
  {
  for (k=2; k< num/2+1; k++)
  if(divisible(num,k))
    return 0;
  return 1;
  /* Returns 1 when 'num' not divisible by 'k' */
  }
}
/* Function 'divisible' is used in function 'prime'.
This gives a perfect top-down approach.*/
```

Output

```
322 <CR>
322 is not prime.
run
79 <CR>
79 is prime.
```

Program 6.5 Write a C program to check the given numbers are prime or not. If the given number is not prime, print the factors. Note: Here the function printfactor() is used to print the factors while executing the function and it does not return any value. *Void* is used when the function is not returning any value and hence the type of the function name is *void*.

```
/* Find out the factors of a given number. */
#include<stdio.h>
int prime();
int divisible();
void printfactor();
void main()
{
 int n;
 scanf("%d", &n);
 if(prime(n))
 printf("%d is prime.",n);
 else
 {
 printf("%d has the following factor/s. ",n);
 printfactor(n);
 }
}
/* printing factors. */
void printfactor(num)
int num;
{
 int k;
/* local variables are declared within the function.
*/
 for (k=2; k< num/2+1; k++)
 if(divisible(num,k))
   printf("%d,",k);
 printf(".\n ");
}
/* Function 'prime' is to be included here, as
given in P6.3.*/
/* Function 'divisible' is used in function 'prime'
and 'printfactor'. This gives a perfect top-down
approach.*/
/* Function 'divisible' is to be included here.*/
```

Function of type *void* does not return any value.

Output

```
7 <CR>
7 is prime.
run
```

```
64 <CR>
64 has the following factor/s. 2,4,8,16,32,.
run
231 <CR>
231 has the following factor/s.
2,3,6,7,11,14,21,22,33,42,66,77,.
```

Program 6.6 Write a C program to print the prime factors, if any.

```
/* Find out the prime factor/s of a given number. */
#include<stdio.h>
void print factors();
int prime();
int divisible();
void main()
{
  int number;
  printf("Input number.\n");
  scanf("%d", &number);
  if(prime(number))
  printf("%d is prime.",number);
  else
  {
  printf("Prime factor/s of %d is/are ",number);
  print factors(number);
  }
  getchar(); getchar();
}
void print factors(num)
int num;
{
  int k;
  for (k=2; k< num/2+1; k++)
  if (divisible(num,k))
    if(prime(k))
       printf("%d ",k);
```

```
}
/* Function 'prime' is to be included here. */
/* Function 'divisible' is to be included here.*/
```

Output

```
Input number.
231 <CR>
Prime factor/s of 231 is/are 3 7 11
run
2310 <CR>
Prime factor/s of 2310 is/are 2 3 5 7 11
run
7 <CR>
7 is prime.
```

Program 6.7 Write a function which returns the last digit of given numbers.

```
int lastdgt(num,divs)
int num,divs;
{
      if((num - num/10*10)== divs)
        return divs;
      else
        return 0;
}
```

Program 6.8 Write a function to find the sum of the digits.

```
int sumdgt(num)
int num;
{
      int sum=0;
      while(num > 0)
      {
      sum = sum + num - num / 10 * 10;
      num = num / 10;
      }
    return sum;
}
```

Program 6.9 Write a main program along with suitable functions to find a buzz number for infinite data inputs.

```
/* Buzz number. If a number divisible by 7, or
the last digit is 7 or the sum of the digits
divisible by 7 is called a Buzz number. */
#include<stdio.h>
int buzz();
int sumdgt();
int lastdgt();
int dvsbl();
void main()
{
  char ch;
  int num;
  ch = scanf("%d", &num);
  while(ch != EOF)
  {
  if(buzz(num))
    printf("%d is a Buzz
number\n",num);
  else
    printf("%d is NOT a
Buzz number\n",num);
  ch = scanf("%d", &num);
  }
  getchar();
}
int buzz(int num)
{
  if(dvsbl(num,7)
|| lastdgt(num,7) ||
  dvsbl(sumdgt(num),7) )
  return 1;
  else
```

Note the easy modular top-down approach in each level. At the top level the logic is very simple, i.e. if the given number is buzz number declare as buzz or declare as NOT a buzz number. The functions can be used in any other applications and thus coding becomes more easy.

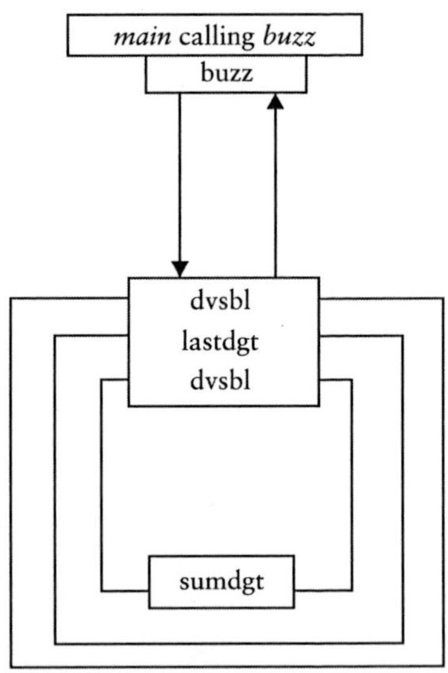

```
  return 0;
}
/* 'dvsbl' has two arguments; In the 1st case
"num" & 7; In the 2nd case 'sum of the digit' of
"num" and 7. */
int dvsbl(num,divs)
int num,divs;
{
  if(num==0)
  return 0;
  if (num/divs*divs == num)
  return divs;
  else
  return 0;
}
int lastdgt(num,divs)
int num,divs;
{
  if((num - num/10*10)== divs)
  return divs;
  else
  return 0;
}
int sumdgt(num)
int num;
{
  int sum=0;
  while(num > 0)
  {
    sum = sum + num - num / 10 * 10;
    num = num / 10;
  }
  return sum;
}
/* Some of the above functions are written else
where also. Repeated for more clarity. */
```

Output

```
789 <CR>
789 is NOT a Buzz number
97 <CR>
97 is a Buzz number
707 <CR>
707 is a Buzz number
700 <CR>
700 is a Buzz number
995 is NOT a Buzz number
86 is a Buzz number
.......^Z <CR>
```

Program 6.10 Write a function which returns the sum of the digits to a single digit with a main program. Example: sum of 674 —> 17 —> 8.

```
#include<stdio.h>
void main()
{
  char ch;
  int num;
  ch = scanf("%d",&num);
  while(ch != EOF)
  {
   printf("sum of %d is %d\n",num,sumdgt(num));
   ch = scanf("%d",&num);
  }
}
int sumdgt(num)
int num;
{
  int sum=num;
  while (num > 9)
  {
   sum = 0;
   do
   {
   printf("num = %d\t",num);
   sum = sum + num - num / 10 * 10;
   num = num / 10;
   }
   while(num > 0);
```

When the given *num* is a single digit integer, this assignment is required.

```
    printf("\t  sum  =  %d\n",sum);
    num  =sum;
    }
    return  sum;
}
```

The intermediate results are shown in the output for visualization of the sequence of execution of the program.

Output

```
6789 <CR>
num  =  6789  num  =  678  num  =  67  num  =  6
                sum  =  30
num  =  30  num  =  3  sum  =  3
sum  of  6789  is  3
5678 <CR>
num  =  5678  num  =  567  num  =  56  num  =  5
                sum  =  26
num  =  26  num  =  2  sum  =  8
sum  of  5678  is  8
9<CR>
sum  of  9  is  9
........^Z  <CR>
```

Program 6.11 Write a program to find the equivalent binary of a decimal integer in the range of –127 to +127 by using suitable functions. Octal equivalent can also be found out with minimum modifications.

```
/* Finding equivalent binary of a decimal number.
This program can be used for finding octal equivalent
just by changing #define BASE 2 by #define BASE 8 */
#include<stdio.h>
#define MAXSIZE 8
#define BASE 2
void convert();
void printary();
void main()
{
  int num,equivalent[MAXSIZE];
  while(scanf("\n %d",&num) != EOF)
  {
  convert(num,equivalent);
```

```
  printary(equivalent);
  }
}
/* The function 'convert' finds the equivalent of 'num'
and returns the result in an array 'equivalent' and
'printary' prints the content of array 'equivalent'.
Function 'convert' retains the sign of the decimal
integer at location 'equivalent[0]'. */
void convert(deci,equivalent)
int deci,equivalent[MAXSIZE];
{
  int index,sign;
  /* Initializing the array. */
  for(index=0; index<MAXSIZE; index++)
  equivalent[index] =0;
  /* 'sign' will be assigned -1 for -ve values &
       1 for +ve values. */
  sign = (deci < 0) ? -1: 1;
  deci = deci*sign;
  index=1;
  while(deci>0)
  {
  equivalent[index++] = deci - deci/BASE*BASE;
  deci = deci/BASE;
  }
  equivalent[0] = sign;
}
/* printing the array. */
void printary(equivalent)
int equivalent[MAXSIZE];
{
  int index=MAXSIZE-1;
  char ch;
  ch = (equivalent[0] == -1) ? '-' : '+';
  printf("%c",ch);
  while(index > 0)
  printf("%d",equivalent[index—]);
  printf("\n");
```

```
}
/* This program can be used for finding the equivalent of any decimal integer between -127 to +127. For higher range, increase the value of MAXSIZE. Terminate the program by entering ^Z or F6 <CR> */
```

Output

```
0 <CR>          -69 <CR>
+0000000        -1000101
4 <CR>          +127 <CR>
+0000100        +1111111
31 <CR>         128 <CR>
+0011111        +0000000 (Wrong result due
                to the limitaion of the
                program)
                ^Z <CR>
```

Program 6.12 Write a program to find a^n.

```
/* base ** power */
#include<stdio.h>
int power();
void main()
{
  int base,powar;
  printf("Input BASE POWER \t");
  scanf("%d %d",&base,&powar);
 printf("%d ** %d = %d",base,powar,power(base,powar));
  getchar();getchar();
}
int power(basee,pwr)
int basee,pwr;
{
  int p,i;
  p = (pwr==0) ? 1 : basee;
  for(i=1; i<pwr; i++)
  p *= basee ;
  return p;
}
/* if pwr == 0 then p = 1 else p = base */
```

Output

```
Input BASE POWER 9 3 <CR>
9 ** 3 = 729 <CR>
```

← *equivalent to* p = p*basee

Program 6.13 Sum of the elements of an array by using recursion.

```
#include<stdio.h>
#define MAX 100
int getSumArray(int a[], int n);
void main()
{
int n, I, a[MAX];
printf("Enter the size of the array: ");
scanf("%d", &n);
printf("\nEnter the array elements\n");
for(i=0; i<n; i++)
scanf("%d", &a[i]);
printf("The sum of array elements = %d",
getSumArray(a,n));
}
int getSumArray(int a[], int n)
{
if(n<0)
return 0;
else
return a[n]+getSumArray(a,n-1);
}
```

Output

```
Enter the size of the array: 5
Enter the array elements
5
3
2
1
4
The sum of array elements = 15
```

Program 6.14 Program to calculate nCr and nPr using functions.

```
#include<stdio.h>
  long factorial(int);
  long find_ncr(int, int);
  long find_npr(int, int);
  void main()
  {
  int n, r;
   long ncr, npr;
     printf("Enter the value of n and r\n");
  scanf("%d%d",&n,&r);
  ncr = find_ncr(n, r);
  npr = find_npr(n, r);
  printf("%dC%d = %ld\n", n, r, ncr);
  printf("%dP%d = %ld\n", n, r, npr);
     }
   long find_ncr(int n, int r) {
   long result;
   result = factorial(n)/(factorial(r)*factorial(n-r));
       return result;
  }
  long find_npr(int n, int r) {
   long result;
  result = factorial(n)/factorial(n-r);
  return result;
  }
  long factorial(int n) {
  int c;
  long result = 1;
  for (c = 1; c <= n; c++)
     result = result*c;
  return result;
  }
```

Output

```
Enter the value of n and r
6
4
6C4 = 15
6P4 = 360
```

Program 6.15 Using function, calculate GCD of any 3 numbers.

```
#include<stdio.h>
  void main(){
  int a,b,c;
  printf(“Enter 3 numbers:”);
  scanf(“%d%d%d”,&a,&b,&c);
   printf(“Greatest Common Divisor is %d”,
gcd(gcd(a,b),c));
  }
  int gcd(long a,long b)
  {
  if(b==0)
  return a;
  else
  return gcd(b,a%b);
  }
```

Output

```
Enter 3 numbers:3 6 12
Greatest Common Divisor is 3
```

Program 6.16 Develop separate C functions to implement a calculator that performs +, –, *, / and % arithmetic algebraic operations on two input numbers. Function names: Read(), Calculate(), Display(). The main function should contain only function calls.

```
#include<stdio.h>
#include<conio.h>
void Read()
{ int m,n;
char c;
printf(“Enter two numbers: ”);
scanf(“%d,%d”,&m,&n);
printf(“Enter the operator: ”);
c=getch();
```

```
}
int calculate(int x,int y,char ch);
{ int result
if(ch=='+')
result=x+y;
if(ch=='-')
result=x-y;
if(ch=='*')
result=x*y;
if(ch=='/')
result=x/y;
if(ch=='%')
result=x%y;
return(result);
}
void display(int r)
{ printf("\nResult=%d",r);
}
void main(){
clrscr();
choice =0;
do{
printf("\n1. Addition\n");
printf("\n2. Subtraction\n");
printf("\n3. Multiplication\n");
printf("\n4. Division\n");
printf("\n5. Modulus\n");
printf("\n6. Exit\n");
printf("\nEnter your choice: ");
scanf("%d",&choice);
while(choice!=6);
Read();
calculate();
display();
getch();
}
```

Output

```
1. Addition
2. Subtraction
3. Multiplication
4. Division
5. Modulus
6. Exit
Enter your choice: 1
Enter two numbers: 3 2
Enter the operator:+
Result=5
Enter your choice:6
```

Program 6.17 Trace of a matrix is the sum of the leading diagonal elements of the matrix. Write a function to obtain the trace of the given matrix of order n x n.

```
#include<stdio.h>
#include<conio.h>
#define MAXROWS 20
#define MAXCOLS 20
void trace(int a[][MAXCOLS],int m)
{ int sum=0,k;
for(k=0;k<m;k++)
sum=sum+a[k][k];
printf("\n\nSum of the diagonal elements of a matrix
is: %d",sum);
}
void main(){
 int a[MAXROWS][MAXCOLS],i,j,n;
 printf("\nEnter the order of matrix: ");
 scanf("%d",&n);
 printf("\nEnter the elements of matrix: ");
 for(i=0;i<n;i++)
 for(j=0;j<n;j++)
 scanf("%d",&a[i][j]);
 printf("\nThe matrix is\n");
 for(i=0;i<n;i++){
 printf("\n");
 for(j=0;j<n;j++){
```

```
printf("%d\t",a[i][j]);
}
}
trace(a,n);
getch();
} }
```

Output

```
Enter the order of matrix:3
Enter the elements of matrix:1 3 4
1 2 4
1 3 3
The matrix is
1 3 4
1 2 4
1 3 3
Sum of the diagonal elements of a matrix
is:6
```

6.7 Summary

In this chapter, we have discussed about function definition, function calling, various methods of calling a function which includes call by value and call by reference, passing arrays to functions and recursive functions. In the next chapter, we will discuss about string handling.

6.8 Review Questions

1. Write the general syntax of a function in C with an example.
2. Write a function SORT that arranges the elements of an array in descending order.
3. Explain call by value and call by reference.
4. What is recursion?
5. How will you pass arrays to a function?
6. What do you mean by function prototype? What is its use?

CHAPTER 7 String Handling

7.1 Introduction

In C programming, array of character are called strings. A string is terminated by null character /0. For example:

```
"Welcome"
```

Here, "Welcome" is a string. When, compiler encounters strings, it appends null character at the end of string.

W	e	l	c	o	m	e	\0

7.2 Declaration of Strings

Strings are declared in C in similar manner as arrays. Only difference is that, strings are of char type.

```
Char s[5];
```

s[0]	s[1]	s[2]	s[3]	s[4]

Strings can also be declared using pointer which will be covered in Chapter 9.

```
Char *p
```

7.3 Initialization of Strings

In C, strings can be initialized in a number of ways.

```
Char c[]="abcd";
        OR,
char c[5]="abcd";
        OR,
char c[]={'a','b','c','d','\0'};
        OR;
char c[5]={'a','b','c','d','\0'};
```

c[0]	c[1]	c[2]	c[3]	c[4]
a	b	c	d	\0

Strings can also be initialized using pointers

```
char *c="abcd";
```

7.4 Reading Strings from User

```
char c[20];
scanf("%s",c);
```

Strings variable *c* can only take a word. It is because when white space is encountered, the scanf() function terminates.

Program 7.1 Write a C program to illustrate how to read string from terminal.

```
#include<stdio.h>
void main()
{
char name[20];
printf("Enter name: ");
scanf("%s",name);
printf("Your name is %s.",name);
getch();
}
```

Output

```
Enter name: Edward John
Your name is Edward.
```

Here, program will ignore John because, scanf() function takes only string before the white space.

7.5 Reading Line of Text

Program 7.2 Write a C program to illustrate read line of text manually.

```
#include<stdio.h>
void main(){
char name[30],ch;
inti=0;
printf(“Enter name: ”);
while(ch!=’\n’)      // terminates if user hit enter
      {
ch=getchar();
name[i]=ch;
i++;
      }
name[i]=’\0’;              // inserting null character
                              at end.
printf(“Name: %s”,name);
getch();
}
```

Output

```
Enter name: Edward John
Name: Edward John
```

This process to take string is tedious. There are predefined functions gets() and puts in C language to read and display string respectively.

Program 7.3 Write a C program to illustrate gets and puts.

```
void main(){
char name[30];
printf(“Enter name: ”);
gets(name);          //Function to read string from
                       user.
printf(“Name: ”);
puts(name);       //Function to display string.
```

```
getch();
}
```

Output

```
Enter name: Edward John
Name: Edward John
```

7.6 Passing Strings to Functions

String can be passed to function in similar manner as arrays as, string is also an array.

Program 7.4 Write a C program to illustrate how strings can be passed to functions.

```
#include<stdio.h>
void Display(char ch[]);
void main(){
char c[50];
printf("Enter string: ");
gets(c);
Display(c);        // Passing string c to function.
getch();
}
void Display(char ch[]){
printf("String Output: ");
puts(ch);
}
```

Output

```
Enter string: Programming in C
String Output: Programming in C
```

Here, string `c` is passed from `main()` function to user-defined function `Display()`. In function declaration, `ch[]` is the formal argument.

7.7 String Handling Functions

We can perform different types of string operations manually like: finding length of string, concatenating (joining) two strings, etc. But, for programmers ease, many library functions are defined under header file `<string.h>` to handle these commonly used tasks in C programming.

Strings are often needed to be manipulated by programmer according to the need of a problem. All string manipulation can be done manually by the programmer but, this makes programming complex and large. To solve this, the C supports a large number of string handling functions.

There are numerous functions defined in "string.h" header file. Few commonly used string handling functions are discussed below:

Function	Description
strlen()	Calculates the length of string
strcpy()	Copies a string to another string
strcat()	Concatenates (joins) two strings
strcmp()	Compares two string
strlwr()	Converts string to lowercase
strupr()	Converts string to uppercase

Strings handling functions are defined under "string.h" header file, i.e., we have to include the code below to run string handling functions.

```
#include<string.h>
```

(a) strlen(): In C, strlen() function calculates the length of string. It takes only one argument, i.e., string name. Function strlen() returns the value of type integer.

Syntax of strlen()

```
temp_variable = strlen(string_name);
```

Program 7.5 Write a C program to calculate the length of a string.

```
/* Program to calculate the length of string*/
#include<stdio.h>
#include<string.h>
void main(){
char a[20]="Program";
```

```
char b[20]={'P','r','o','g','r','a','m','\0'};
char c[20];
printf("Enter string: ");
gets(c);
printf("Length of string a=%d \n",strlen(a));
//calculates the length of string before null
character.
printf("Length of string b=%d \n",strlen(b));
printf("Length of string c=%d \n",strlen(c));
getch();
}
```

Output

```
Enter string: String
Length of string a=7
Length of string b=7
Length of string c=7
```

(b) strcpy(): Function strcpy() copies the content of one string to the content of another string. It takes two arguments.

Syntax of strcpy()

```
strcpy(destination,source);
```

Here, source and destination are both the name of the string. This statement, copies the content of string source to the content of string destination.

Program 7.6 Write a C program to copy the contents of a string.

```
#include<stdio.h>
#include<string.h>
void main(){
char a[10],b[10];
printf("Enter string: ");
gets(a);
strcpy(b,a);//Contents of string a is copied to
              string b.
printf("Copied string: ");
puts(b);
getch();
}
```

Output

```
Enter string:  C Programming
Copied string: C Programming
```

(c) **strcat():** In C programming, strcat() concatenates (joins) two strings. It takes two arguments, i.e., two strings and resultant string is stored in the first string specified in the argument.

Syntax of strcat()

```
strcat(first_string,second_string);
```

Program 7.7 Write a C program to concatenates two strings.

```
#include<stdio.h>
#include<string.h>
void main(){
char str1[]="This is ", str2[]="programming";
strcat(str1,str2);//concatenates str1 and str2 and
                  resultant string is stored in str1.
puts(str1);
puts(str2);
getch();
}
```

Output

```
This is programming
Programming
```

(d) **strcmp():** In C programming, strcmp() compares two string and returns value 0, if the two strings are equal. Function strcmp() takes two arguments, i.e., name of two string to compare.

Syntax of strcmp()

```
temp_variable=strcmp(string1,string2);
```

Program 7.8 Write a C program to compare two strings.

```
#include<stdio.h>
#include<string.h>
void main(){
```

```
char str1[30],str2[30];
printf(“Enter first string: “);
gets(str1);
printf(“Enter second string: “);
gets(str2);
if(strcmp(str1,str2)==0)
printf(“Both strings are equal”);
else
printf(“Strings are unequal”);
getch();
}
```

Output

```
Enter first string: Apple
Enter second string: Apple
Both strings are equal.
```

If two strings are not equal, strcmp() returns positive value if ASCII value of first mismatching element of first string is greater than that of second string and negative value if ASCII value of first mismatching element of first string is less than that of second string. For example:

```
char str1[]=”and”,str2[]=”cat”;
temp=strcmp(str1,str2);
```

Since, ASCII value of ‘a’ is less than that of ‘c’, variable temp will be negative.

(e) **strlwr():** In C programming, strlwr() function converts all the upper-case characters in that string to lower-case characters. The resultant from strlwr() is stored in the same string. Function strlwr() leaves the lower-case characters as it is and converts upper-case characters to lower case.

Syntax of strlwr()

```
strlwr(string_name);
```

Program 7.9 Write a C program to convert all characters in a string to lower case.

```
#include<stdio.h>
#include<string.h>
void main(){
char str1[]=”Lower Case”;
```

```
puts(strlwr(str1));//converts to lower case and
displays it.
getch();
}
```

Output

```
lower case
```

(f) **strupr():** In C programming, strupr() function converts all the lower-case characters in that string to upper-case characters. The resultant from strupr() is stored in the same string. Function strupr() leaves the upper-case characters as it is and converts lower-case characters to upper case.

Syntax of strupr()

```
strupr(string_name);
```

Program 7.10 Write a C program to convert all characters in a string to upper case.

```
#include<stdio.h>
#include<string.h>
void main(){
char str1[]="Upper Case";
puts(strupr(str1));//Converts to upper case and
displays it.
return 0;
}
```

Output

```
Upper Case
```

7.8 Solved Programs

Program 7.11 Program to do the linear search of any one particular character on an array of elements. Display if found or not found, if found display its position also.

```
#include<stdio.h>
#include<conio.h>
```

```
void main()
{int i=0,count=0;
char h;
char s[20];
clrscr();
// read all whitespace,then store all characters
up to a newline
printf(“Enter a line of text\n”);
scanf(“ %[^\n]”,s);
printf(“Enter a character to be searched\n”);
scanf(“%c”,&h);//store a character
while((s[i]=getchar())!=’\0’)
{
if(s[i]==h)
  {
  printf(“Character %c is found at location %d”,
h,i);
     count++;
  }
i++;
}
if(count==0)
printf(“Character not found in array”);
}
```

Output

```
Enter a line of text
Apples are red
Enter a character to be searched
Z
Character not found in array
```

Program 7.12 C program to sort N strings.

```
#include<stdio.h>
#include<string.h>
 void main() {
    char s[5][20], t[20];
    int i, j,n;
    clrscr();
     printf(“\nEnter the number of strings to be
sorted : “);
```

```
      scanf(“%d”,&n);
    for (i = 0; i < n; i++)
      scanf(“%s”, s[i]);
      for (i = 1; i < n; i++) {
          for (j = 1; j < n; j++) {
                if (strcmp(s[j - 1], s[j]) > 0) {
                      strcpy(t, s[j - 1]);
                      strcpy(s[j - 1], s[j]);
                      strcpy(s[j], t);
                }
          }
    }
      printf(“\nStrings in order are : ”);
    for (i = 0; i < n; i++)
          printf(“\n%s”, s[i]);
      getch();
}
```

Output

```
Enter the number of strings to be sorted:5
mango
orange
apple
pear
grapes
Strings in order are:
apple
grapes
mango
orange
pear
```

Program 7.13 Write a C program to check whether a string is a palindrome or not.

```
#include<stdio.h>
#include<string.h>
void main(){
char string1[20];
int i,length,flag=0;
printf(“Enter a string: ”);
scanf(“%s”,string1);
length=strlen(string1);
```

```
for(i=0;i<length;i++)
{
if(string1[i]!=string1[length-i-1])
{flag=1;
break;
}
}
if(flag==1)
printf("%s is not a Palindrome",string1);
else
printf("%s is a Palindrome",string1);
}
```

Output

```
Enter a string:abba
abba is a Palindrome
```

Program 7.14 Write a 'C' program to read a line of text and count the number of vowels consonants, digits and blank spaces.

```
#include<stdio.h>
      void main(){
      char line[150];
      int i,v,c,d,s;
      v=c=d=s=0;
      printf("Enter a line of string:\n");
      scanf("%[^\n]",line);
      for(i=0;line[i]!='\0';++i)
      {
                  if(line[i]=='a' || line[i]=='e'
|| line[i]=='i' || line[i]=='o' || line[i]=='u'
|| line[i]=='A' || line[i]=='E' || line[i]=='I' ||
line[i]=='O' || line[i]=='U')
             ++v;
     else if((line[i]>='a'&& line[i]<='z') ||
(line[i]>='A'&& line[i]<='Z'))
             ++c;
    else if(line[i]>='0'&&c<='9')
```

```
                ++d;
          else if (line[i]==' ')
                ++s;
        }
        printf("Vowels: %d",v);
        printf("\nConsonants: %d",c);
        printf("\nDigits: %d",d);
        printf("\nWhite spaces: %d",s);
        getch();
}
```

Output

```
Enter a line of string:
Apples are red.
Vowels: 5
Consonants: 7
Digits: 0
White spaces: 2
```

Program 7.15 Write a program to copy a string from one string to another. (without using stropy)

```
#include<stdio.h>
#include<conio.h>
void main()
{
int i=0;
char s1[10],s2[10];
clrscr();
printf("\n enter the string 1 \n");
gets(s1);
while(s1[i]!=NULL)
{
s2[i]=s1[i];
i++;
}
s2[i]='\0';
printf("\n After copy the string1= %s",s1);
printf("\n After copy the string2= %s",s2);
getch();
}
```

Output

```
Enter the string 1
Program
After copy the string 1 = Program
After copy the string 2 = Program
```

Program 7.16 Write a program to concatenate two strings into a new string.

```
#include<stdio.h>
#include<string.h>
void main() {
    char str1[100];
    char str2[100];
    char str3[100];
     int len;
     printf("\nEnter the String 1 : ");
     gets(str1);
     printf("\nEnter the String 2 : ");
     gets(str2);
    strcpy(str3, str1);
    strcat(str3, str2);
    printf("\nConcatenated String : %s", str3);
    getch();
  }
```

Output

```
Enter the String 1: Program
Enter the String 2: Logic
Concatenated String: Program logic
```

Program 7.17 Write an interactive C program to find the longest word in a given sentence and print the longest word.

```
#include<stdio.h>
      #include<conio.h>
      #include<string.h>
      void main()
      {     char a[50],b[20],c[20];
            int i,j=0,l=0;
```

```
clrscr();
printf("Enter a string:\n");
gets(a);
for(i=0;i<=strlen(a);i++)
{if(a[i]!=32 && a[i]!='\0')
      b[j++]=a[i];
      else
      {b[j]='\0';
            if(strlen(b)>l)
            { strcpy(c,b);
                  l=strlen(b);
            }
            j=0;
      }
}
printf("The longest word is:");
puts(c);
getch();      }
```

Output

```
Enter a string: Knowledge is power
The longest word is:Knowledge
```

Program 7.18 Write a function that will scan a character string passed as an argument and convert all lower-case letters into their upper-case equivalents.

```
#include<stdio.h>
#include<string.h>
void toupper(char s[]);
void main(){
   char str[20];
   printf("Enter any string->");
   scanf("%s",str);
   printf("The string is->%s",str);
toupper(str);
getch();
```

```
}
void toupper(char str[]){
int i;
   for(i=0;i<=strlen(str);i++){
                   if(str[i]>=97&&str[i]<=122)
                   str[i]=str[i]-32;
   }
   printf("\nThe string in lowercase is->%s”,str);
   }
```

Output

```
Enter any string ->APPLES are RED
The string is -> APPLES are RED
The string in lower case is ->apples are
```

7.9 Summary

This chapter gives an overview of strings and various functions associated with strings to manipulate it. We will discuss structure and union in the next chapter.

7.10 Review Questions

1. What is the null character and what it is used for in the context of strings?
2. Write a program to check whether a string is palindrome or not.
3. Write a program to find the longest word in a sentence and print the longest word.
4. Write a function that will scan a character string passed as an argument and convert all lower-case letters to upper-case letters.
5. Explain sorting of strings in detail.
6. Write a program to copy a string from one string to another.
7. Write a program to concatenate two strings into a new string.

8. Write a program to find the number of characters in a string using pointers.
9. Write a C program to read a line of text and count the number of vowels, consonants, digits and blank spaces.
10. Explain in detail, the different string related operations and the string handling functions with suitable example programs to demonstrate each of them.

CHAPTER

8

Structure and Union

8.1 Introduction to Structure

Structure in C is a mechanism to store heterogeneous data. We have already studied *array* as a mechanism to store homogeneous data. So structure is a mechanism method to keep related information together. Heterogeneous data are stored in a way by keeping different related variables in a structure. In C structure is mechanism to define a real world object. The variables in a structure are called *members*.

Managing heterogeneous yet related data are important in a program. For example, if we need to define a real world object, say a student. We know a student has number of properties like name, id, age, class, address, etc. We can use the structure to define a student by keeping these properties. This is also one way to define *user defined data types*. We use the keyword *struct* to define a student.

```
struct  student
{
  char  name[20];
```

```
    int id;
    int age;
    char class[10];
    char address[30];
  };
```

So by using the keyword *struct*, it tells to the compiler that a structure *student* is being declared. Notice that the declaration is terminated by a semicolon. Also by this statement we now defined a new data type name *student*. The declaration can be thought of as a template; that is *no variable is created and no storage is allocated*. So after defining a new type, the type *student* can be used as same as any other variable. That is we can now declare a variable of the type *student*. This can be done by

```
struct student student_1;
```

where *struct student* is the data type and *student_1* is a variable. This declaration allocates sufficient memory to accommodate all of its members. The size of a structure variable is the total aggregate size of all the members in that structure. So in the above declaration, total of 64 byte memory need to allocated for the variable *student_1*. An alternative method to declare variable is to write

```
struct student
{
  char name[20];
  int id;
  int age;
  char class[10];
  char address[30];
} student_1, student_2;
```

which defines the type *struct student* and declares *student_1* and *student_2* to be of this type, all at the same time. Here, it is important to note that both *student_1* and *student_2* contains all the five members and these two variables are said to the two instances of the type *struct student*.

If you only need one structure variable, the structure name is not needed. That is this

```
struct
{char name[20];
 int id;
 int age;
 char class[10];
 char address[30];
} student_1;
```

declares one variable named *student_1*. Since there is no type name explicitly given hereafter no further variable cannot be declared.

8.2 Accessing Structure Members

The individual members of a structure are accessed using a member access operator "." (usually called as *dot operator*). To assign a value to *id* member of the structure variable *student_1*, we can write

```
student_1.id = 10;
```

The general form is *structure_variable.member_name*.

8.3 Structure Assignment

If we have two structure variable of same type we can assign the values of one variable to another variable through a single structure assignment. For an example the statement

```
student_1 = student_2;
```

cause each member of *student_1* to be assigned the values of the corresponding member of *student_2*.

Program 8.1 Write a simple program to store values to a structure and print the result.

```
#include<stdio.h>
#include<conio.h>
void main()
{
 struct abc
 {
 int a;
 float b;
 char c;
```

```
  }struct1;
  clrscr();
  //to store value to the structure
  printf("\nEnter character value");
  scanf("%c",&struct1.c);
  printf("\nEnter an integer value");
  scanf("%d",&struct1.a);
  printf("\nEnter a float value");
  scanf("%f",&struct1.b);
  // to print the values from the structure
  printf("The Values you entered to the structure
are\n");
  printf("%c %d %f",struct1.c,struct1.a,struct1.b);
  getch();
}
```

Output

```
The result is as per the user input,
this is only a dummy result
'T' 23 45.7
```

The Structure can be initialized during its declaration is demonstrated in the next example.

Program 8.2 Write a program to initialize a structure at its declaration time and print the result.

```
#include<stdio.h>
#include<conio.h>
void main()
{
  struct abc
  {
  char c;
  int a;
  float b;
  }struct1={'T',34,45.7};
  clrscr();
  printf("%c %d %f",struct1.c,struct1.a,struct1.b);
  getch();
}
```

Output

```
T 34 45.7
```

Program 8.3 Write a program to declare multiple structure variables, initialize them and print the result.

```
#include<stdio.h>
#include<conio.h>
void main()
{
 struct student
 {
 char name[10];
 int age;
 float fees;
 };
struct student
={"Sunil",22,655.50},student2={"Anil",23,624.75};
 clrscr();
printf("%s  %d  %.2f",student1.name,student1.age,
student1.fees);
printf("\n%s  %d  %.2f",student2.name,student2.age,
student2.fees);
 getch();
 }
```

Output

```
Sunil 22 655.50
Anil 23 624.75
```

A structure can be declared and initialized globally. The effect of doing this is that we can access the structure in the main program as well as in the sub programs and functions. This is explained in the next example.

Program 8.4 Program to demonstrate the global declaration of structure and its use in functions.

```
#include<stdio.h>
#include<conio.h>
```

```
struct student
  {
  char name[10];
  int age;
  float fees;
  };
struct student student1={"sunil",22,655.50},student2
={"anil",23,624.75};
void display();
void main()
{
  clrscr();
   printf("%s  %d  %.2f",student1.name,student1.
age,student1.fees);
   printf("\n%s  %d  %.2f",student2.name,student2.
age,student2.fees);
  display();
  getch();
  }
  void display()
  {
   printf("\n%s  %d  %.2f",student1.name,student1.
age,student1.fees);
   printf("\n%s  %d  %.2f",student2.name,student2.
age,student2.fees);
  }
```

Output

```
Sunil  22  655.50 } Result of structure printed
Anil  23  624.75  } by main program
Sunil  22  655.50 } Result of structure printed
Anil  23  624.75  } through function
```

Program 8.5 Write a program to compare two structures using comparison operators and print the result.

```
#include<stdio.h>
#include<conio.h>
#include<string.h>
void main()
{
```

```
struct abc
{
char name[10];
int a;
float b;
};
struct abc b1={"computer",23,45.62},b2;
clrscr();
b2=b1;
printf("%s %d %f",b2.name,b2.a,b2.b);
if(strcmp(b1.name,b2.name)==0&&b1.a==b2.a&&b1.
b==b2.b)
printf("\nBoth structures have the same values");
else
printf("\nBoth structures have different values");
/*if(b1==b2)
 printf("\nBoth structures have the same values");
if(b1!=b2)
 printf("\nBoth structures have different values");*/
getch();
}
```

Output

```
Computer 23 45.62
```

Note: In the above program there are multiple commented statements. Why it is kept like that is because some of the compilers do not support such a comparison. So we can bypass this problem by comparing the structure in the above manner.

8.4 Arrays and Structures

Having defined a structure, we can declare arrays of structures too. To obtain an array of 10 students, we need write it like this

```
sturct student stud[10];
```

This creates 10 set of variables that are organized as defined in the structure *student*.

Program 8.6 Write a program to create array of structure variables to store the details of two students and print the result.

```
#include<stdio.h>
#include<conio.h>
void main()
{
  struct student
  {
  char name[10];
  int age;
  float fees;
  };
   struct  student  s1[2]={{“aby”,26,34.5},
{“anil”,32,50.2}};
  int i;
  clrscr();
  for(i=0;i<2;i++)
  {
 printf(“\n%s %d %.2f”,s1[i].name,s1[i].age, s1[i].
fees);
  }
  getch();
}
```

Output

```
aby  26  34.5
anil  32  50.2
```

a	b	y	\0							26	34.5
a	n	i	l	\0						32	50.2

8.5 Structure within Structures

Structure within structures are otherwise known as nested structures. The peculiarity of this is we can easily enclose a structure within another structure. We know that a structure is a *group of heterogeneous* data types.

8.6 Unions

A *union*, like structure, is a user defined data type. By *union*, C gives a convenient mechanism to share a memory location between two or more different types of variables. The programmer is responsible for interpreting the stored values correctly. Declaring a *union* is similar to structure declaration.

```
union student
{
  char name[20];
  int id;
  int age;
  char class[10];
  char address[30];
};
```

Now a new data type is defined. We can declare variable for a union data type by writing

```
union student student_1;
```

In *student_1*, every variable share a common memory. That is, when a *union* variable is declared, the compiler automatically allocates enough memory to accommodate the largest member of union. It should be noted that the size of the variable *student_1* is not the total aggregate size of the members as like in the structure. Since it allocates only the highest possible sized variable, the size of *union* variable has the size equivalent to size of the highest sized variable. The members of the *union* variable can be accessed as same as the structure variable using *dot operator*. The following Table 8.1 shows the difference between structure and union.

Table 8.1: Comparison of Structure and Union.

Structure	Union
1. The keyword struct is used to define a structure.	1. The keyword union is used to define a union.
2. When a variable is associated with a structure, the compiler allocates the memory for each member.	2. When a variable is associated with a union, the compiler allocates the memory by considering the

The size of structure is greater than or equal to the sum of sizes of its members.	size of the largest memory. So, size of union is equal to the size of largest member.
3. Each member within a structure is assigned unique storage area of location.	3. Memory allocated is shared by individual members of union.
4. The address of each member will be in ascending order. This indicates that memory for each member will start at different offset values.	4. The address is same for all the members of a union. This indicates that every member begins at the same offset value.
5. Altering the value of a member will not affect other members of the structure.	5. Altering the value of any of the member will alter other member values.

8.7 Solved Programs

Program 8.7 C program to read in the names and marks of 5 subjects of 10 students. The result should be displayed as "Fail" if the average mark is less than 40%.

```
#include<stdio.h>
#include<conio.h>
void main()
{
int i;
struct stud{
char name[20];
int m1,m2,m3,m4,m5;
int total;
float avg;
char grade[20];
} s[10];
printf("Enter the names and marks of 5 subjects\n");
for(i=0;i<10;i++){
printf("Enter the name: ");
scanf("%s",s[i].name);
printf("\nEnter mark1: ");
```

```
scanf(“%d”,&s[i].m1);
printf(“\nEnter mark2: “);
scanf(“%d”,&s[i].m2);
printf(“\nEnter mark3: “);
scanf(“%d”,&s[i].m3);
printf(“\nEnter mark4: “);
scanf(“%d”,&s[i].m4);
printf(“\nEnter mark5: “);
scanf(“%d”,&s[i].m5);
s[i].total=s[i].m1+s[i].m2+s[i].m3+s[i].m4+s[i].m5;
s[i].avg=s[i].total/5;
 if(s[i].avg<40)
strcpy(s[i].grade,”Fail”);
else
strcpy(s[i].grade,”Pass”);
}
printf(“The Result\n”);
printf(“Name\tMark1\tMark2\tMark3\tMark4\tMark5\
tTotal\t\Grade\n”);
for(i=0;i<10;i++)
printf(“%s\t%d\t%d\t%d\t%d\t%d\t%d\t%s\n”,s[i].
name,s[i]. m1,s[i].m2,s[i].m3,s[i].m4,s[i].m5,s[i].
total,s[i].grade);
getch();
}
```

Output

```
Enter the names and marks of 5 subjects
Enter the name:Albert
Enter mark1:12
Enter mark2:35
Enter mark3:89
Enter mark4:65
Enter mark5:68 and so on
```

Program 8.8 C program that reads several different names, addresses, age, qualification and rearranges the names into alphabetic order and then write out the list in the alphabetic order using structure variation within the program.

```
#include<stdio.h>
struct n{
char name[10][10];
```

```
char address[10][10];
int age;
char qual[10][10];
}list[100],t;
void main()
{
int k,i,j;
clrscr();
printf("Enter the number of items in the list:");
scanf("%d",&k);
printf("\nEnter the list\n");
for(i=0;i<k;i++)
{
printf("\nName:");
scanf("%s",list[i].name);
printf("\nAddress: " );
scanf("%s",list[i].address);
flushall();
printf("\nAge: ");
scanf("%d",&list[i].age);
printf("\nQualification: ");
scanf("%s",list[i].qual);
}
for(i=0;i<k-1;i++){
for(j=i+1;j<k;j++)
{
if((strcmp(list[i].name,list[j].name))>0)
t=list[i];
list[i]=list[j];
list[j]=t;
}
}
printf("\n\tName\tAddress\tAge\tQualification\n");
for(i=0;i<k;i++)
{
printf("\n\t%s",list[i].name);
printf("\t%s",list[i].address);
```

```
printf("\t%d",list[i].age);
printf("\t%s",list[i].qual);
}
getch();
}
```

Output

```
Enter the number of items in the list:2
Enter the list
Name: Smith
Address: New Road
Age:30
Qualification: MS
Name: Adams
Address: Old Road
Age:30
Qualification: MS
Name     Address      Age    Qualification
Adams    Old Road     30     MS
Smith    New Road     30     MS
```

Program 8.9 Declare a structure to represent complex number. Write a program to add, subtract, multiply and divide two complex numbers.

```
#include<stdio.h>
#include<math.h>
#include<conio.h>
struct comp
{
 double realpart;
 double imgpart;
}w1,w2,w;
void main()
{
 int opern=0;
 clrscr();
do{
 printf("\n\n \t\t\t***** MAIN MENU *****");
 printf("\n\n Select your option: \n 1 : ADD\n 2
: SUBTRACT\n 3 :MULTIPLY\n 4 :DIVIDE\n 0 : EXIT
\n\n\t\t Enter your Option [ ]\b\b");
 scanf("%d",&opern);
 switch(opern)
```

```
  {
  case 0:
  exit(0);
  case 1:
  {
  printf("\n Enter two Complex Numbers (x+iy):\n
Real Part of First Number:");
  scanf("%lf",&w1.realpart);
  printf("\n Imaginary Part of First Number:");
  scanf("%lf",&w1.imgpart);
  printf("\n Real Part of Second Number:");
  scanf("%lf",&w2.realpart);
  printf("\n Imaginary Part of Second Number:");
  scanf("%lf",&w2.imgpart);
  w.realpart = w1.realpart+w2.realpart;
  w.imgpart = w1.imgpart+w2.imgpart;
printf("\n Answer = %lf+%lfi",w.realpart,w.imgpart);
break;
}
  case 2:
  {
  printf("\n Enter two Complex Numbers (x+iy):\n
Real Part of First Number:");
  scanf("%lf",&w1.realpart);
  printf("\n Imaginary Part of First Number:");
  scanf("%lf",&w1.imgpart);
  printf("\n Real Part of Second Number:");
  scanf("%lf",&w2.realpart);
  printf("\n Imaginary Part of Second Number:");
  scanf("%lf",&w2.imgpart);
  w.realpart = w1.realpart-w2.realpart;
  w.imgpart = w1.imgpart-w2.imgpart;
printf("\n Answer = %lf+%lfi",w.realpart,w.imgpart);
break;
}
  case 3:
{
  printf("\n Enter two Complex Numbers (x+iy):\n
Real Part of First Number:");
  scanf("%lf",&w1.realpart);
```

```
  printf("\n  Imaginary  Part  of  First  Number:");
  scanf("%lf",&w1.imgpart);
  printf("\n  Real  Part  of  Second  Number:");
  scanf("%lf",&w2.realpart);
  printf("\n  Imaginary  Part  of  Second  Number:");
  scanf("%lf",&w2.imgpart);
 w.realpart=(w1.realpart*w2.realpart)-(w1.imgpart*w2.
imgpart);
  w.imgpart=(w1.realpart*w2.imgpart)+(w1.imgpart*w2.
realpart);
 printf("\n Answer = %lf+%lfi",w.realpart,w.imgpart);
  break;
}
case  4:
printf("\n Enter two Complex Numbers (x+iy):\n Real
Part  of  First  Number:");
  scanf("%lf",&w1.realpart);
  printf("\n  Imaginary  Part  of  First  Number:");
  scanf("%lf",&w1.imgpart);
  printf("\n  Real  Part  of  Second  Number:");
  scanf("%lf",&w2.realpart);
  printf("\n  Imaginary  Part  of  Second  Number:");
  scanf("%lf",&w2.imgpart);
 w.realpart= (w1.realpart*w2.realpart + w1.imgpart*w2.
imgpart)/(w2.realpart*w2.realpart+w2.imgpart*w2.
imgpart);
 w.imgpart = (w1.imgpart*w2.realpart - w1.realpart*w2.
imgpart)/(w2.realpart*w2.realpart  +  w2.imgpart*w2.
imgpart);
 printf("\n Answer = %lf+%lfi",w.realpart,w.imgpart);
  break;
}
}while(opern!=0);
}
```

Output

```
******Main  Menu*****
Select  your  option:
  1:ADD
  2:SUBTRACT
  3:MULTIPLY
  4:DIVIDE
```

```
0:EXIT
Enter your Option []1
Enter two Complex Numbers
Real Part of First Number:3
Imaginary Part of First Number:2
Real Part of Second Number:4
Imaginary Part of Second Number:3
Answer=7+5i
```

Program 8.10 Write a program to add given number of days to a given data(date). Make use of structures wherever possible.

```
#include<stdio.h>
#include<conio.h>
struct daycount
{
  int day;
  int month;
  int year;
};
void main()
{
  struct daycount p;
  int normalyear[] = {31, 28, 31, 30, 31, 30, 31,
31, 30, 31, 30, 31};
  int leapyear[] = {31, 29, 31, 30, 31, 30, 31,
31, 30, 31, 30, 31};
  clrscr();
  p.day = 0;
  p.month = 0;
  p.year = 0;
  printf("Enter the day month and year :\n");
  scanf("%d",&p.day);
  scanf("%d",&p.month);
  scanf("%d",&p.year);
  int day1 = p.day, month1 = p.month, year1 =
p.year, count = 0, value;
  printf("Enter the day count \n");
  scanf("%d",&value);
```

```
  int j = day1, i = month1;
  while(count <= value)
  {
  while((i <= 12) && (count <= value))
  {
    if (year1 % 4 == 0)
    {
   while((j <= leapyear[i - 1]) && (count <= value))
    {
        count++;
        day1 = j;
        j++;
    }
    j = 1;
    month1 = i;
    i++;
    }
    else
    {
    while((j <= normalyear[i - 1]) && (count <=
value))
    {
        count++;
        day1 = j;
        j++;
    }
    j = 1;
    month1 = i;
    i++;
    }
  }
  if(i > 12)
  {
    year1++;
  }
  i = 1;
  }
  p.day = day1;
  p.month = month1;
```

```
  p.year  =  year1;
  printf("The  new  day  is  %d  -  %d  -  %d",p.day,p.
month,p.year);
  getch();
}
```

Output

```
Enter the day month and year :22 12 2015
Enter the day count 3
The new day is 25 - 12 - 2015
```

8.8 Summary

In this chapter, we have presented the structures, how to access structure members, structure assignment, arrays and structures, structure within structures and unions.

8.9 Review Questions

1. What is a structure? How does it differ from an array?
2. Describe the syntax for defining the composition of a structure of individual members be initialized within a structure type declaration.
3. Define and declare a structure to store date, which includes day, month, year.
4. How is an array of structures initialized?
5. How to define a union in C?
6. What is a union? How is it different from a structure?
7. Write a structure specification that includes four float variables called length, breadth, height and volume. Call this structure "box".
8. Compare structure and union with suitable examples.
9. Explain with suitable example the method of sending an entire structure as a parameter to a function.

CHAPTER 9

Pointers

9.1 Introduction

Pointers are one main feature of C language. This gives us a very powerful way of dealing memory. Pointers are considered to be a very powerful tool in C language. These are much more commonly used in C than in many other languages. In this chapter, we will make a thorough look about pointers. A variable is a memory position where we can store values. Programs use memory for storing instructions as well as the values of the variables that comes in the program. Each byte in the memory has its own memory address. The memory address may be a number to represent the exact position. The numbers start at 0 and grow according to the size of the RAM. The fact is that, there will be 16 million positions in the memory if we have a memory of about 16 MB.

What are pointers mentioned for? And common reasons of using pointers;

- Accessing Array elements (and accessing variables defined outside the function).
- Passing arrays and strings to functions.
- Accelerate speed and reduce complexities of some routines.
- Give the flexibility to change the calling arguments through 'call by reference'.
- Handling dynamic structures like linked lists, trees, graphs, etc.

We will be giving more details of the above uses in more detail in the preceding sections to follow.

9.2 Pointer Variable

A variable which can store memory address of other variable is known as *pointer.* By storing the memory address of other variable, we can say that the first variable (i.e. *pointer variable*) *points* to the second variable. The Asterisk Sign '*' (unary operator) in front of the variable name while declaring says that the variable is a pointer variable. The general form of a pointer variable declaration is

```
type *variable_name;
```

where *type* is any basic types like *int, char*, etc. or complex types like array, structures, etc.

Consider that we are declaring a variable by the command,

```
int amount;
```

Here by this command we are asking the compiler to declare a variable named *amount* and reserve 2 byte space for that variable to store an *integer* type value. We actually don't bother about the exact address of the variable.

```
int amount =79;
```

This statement asks the compiler to find a location (2 byte) in the memory named *amount* and store the value 79 in that location. Here, suppose the memory address is considered to be 1000. Figure 9.1 shows a sample of system memory to explain in this case.

Note: There is no such restriction that when we declare more than one variable it must be in a sequential manner in the memory.

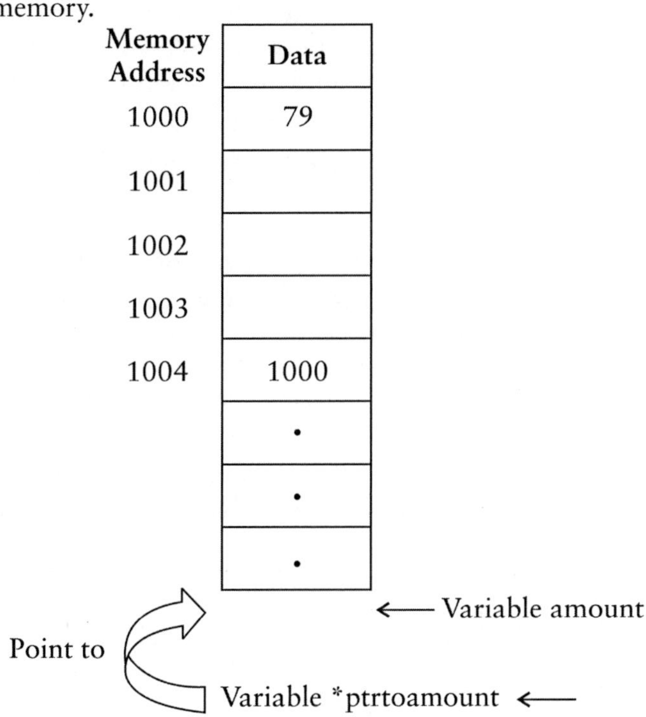

Fig. 9.1: System Memory

Here in this program the variable *quantity* is always linked with the memory address 1000. We can access this value by either giving its name (i.e. *amount)* or its address (i.e. 1000). Since the memory address are integers/hexadecimals, we can store it in any other variables and can use later. Now we will be using a pointer variable to store the address of the variable *amount*.

9.3 Pointer Assignments

By using the above general declaration we can now declare a pointer variable to point to the variable *amount*. This can be done by

```
int *ptrtoamount;
```

declaring the variable *ptrtoamount* is a pointer variable of type *int*. The the type *int*, we declare that the variable *ptrtoamount* has to point to an *integer* type. In our case this is true, because we need to point to a variable *amount*, which is of type *integer*.

Now we can use '&' (unary operator) to assign the address of the variable *amount* to the pointer variable *ptrtoamount*. This is done by

```
ptrtoamount = &amount;
```

The '&' operator if used in front of the variable *amount* is indent to retrieve the address of the corresponding variable. By this assignment statement the pointer variable *ptrtoamount* will contain the value *1000* (i.e. the address of the variable *amount*) and now the first variable is said to point to the second variable.

Note: The actual location of the variable is system dependant and therefore the address of the variable is not known to us.

A Simple Pointer Problem:

Program 9.1 Write a simple program to print the value and address of a variable.

```
#include<stdio.h>
#include<conio.h>
void main()
{
int a=10;
printf("The value of A is %d", a);
printf("The Address where the value 10 is stored
%u" , &a);
getch();
}
```

Output

```
The value and memory address of variable a.
```

A short program to print the memory address of the variables:

Program 9.2 Program to print address of variables.

```
#include<stdio.h>
#include<conio.h>
void main()
{int var1, var2,var3;
printf("The address of variables is %u, %u, %u",
&var1, &var2, &var3);
getch();
}
```

Output

```
The memory address of variables var1,
var2, var3
```

Let's check this solution:

Program 9.3 Program to print the value, address of the variable and address of pointer.

```
#include<stdio.h>
#include<conio.h>
void main()
{int a;
int *b;
a=10; b=&a;
printf("The value of a %d",a);
printf("The Address of a %u",&a);
printf("The Memory address of b %u",&b);
getch();
}
```

Output

```
The value of a 10.
The address of a 1000 (here 1000 is
assumed to be the address of a).
The memory address of b 2000(2000 is
assumed to be the address of b).
```

```
printf("The value of a %d",a); → Prints the content
in the variable a
printf("The Address of a %u",&a); → Prints the
address of variable a
printf("The Memory address of b%u",&b); → Prints
the address of the pointer variable b.
```

Note: Actually the address occupied by the variables in the program depend on many factors like,

- The Operating System
- The Computer
- Other applications running on the same computer.

There are only a few chances to get the same memory address when you run the same program again in the same machine, which means the system allocates the address dynamically.

Value at Address of Operator (Indirection Operator)

Another operator that can use in the pointer assignment is '*' (unary operator) and called as *indirection operator.* The concept is that once we have a pointer variable and an address has been assigned to that pointer, we can access/ change the value of the variable using pointers. For example, since *ptrtoamount* contains the memory address of the variable *amount*, the following statement

```
Netamount = *ptrtoamount;
```

store the value 79 to *Netamount.* Here the operator '*' does is to get the value from the variable, *ptrtoamount* is pointing to, that is the variable *amount.*

Program 9.4 A simple program demonstrating indirection operator.

```
#include<stdio.h>
#include<conio.h>
void main()
{
  int a=5,c;
  int *b;
  b=&a;
  c=*b;
  printf("Value of a=%d",a);
  printf("\nValue of b=%u",b);
  printf("\nValue of a=%d",*b);
  printf("\nAddress of b=%u",&b);
```

```
printf("\nValue of c=%d",c);
getch();
}
```

Output

```
Value of a = 5
Value of b = 5000
Value of a = 5
Address of b = 5000
Value of c = 5
```

Note the sequence of operations by executing the above statements:

(1) *Int a = 5, c*

(2) *int * b*

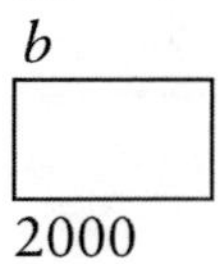

(3) *b = &a;*

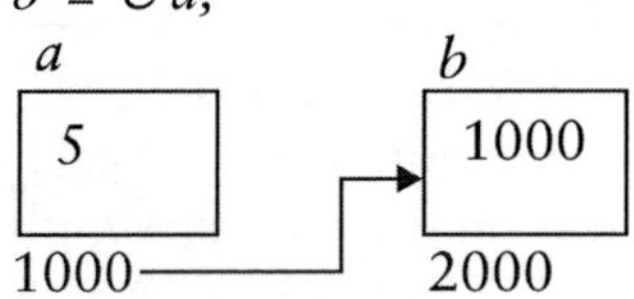

(4) *c = *b;*

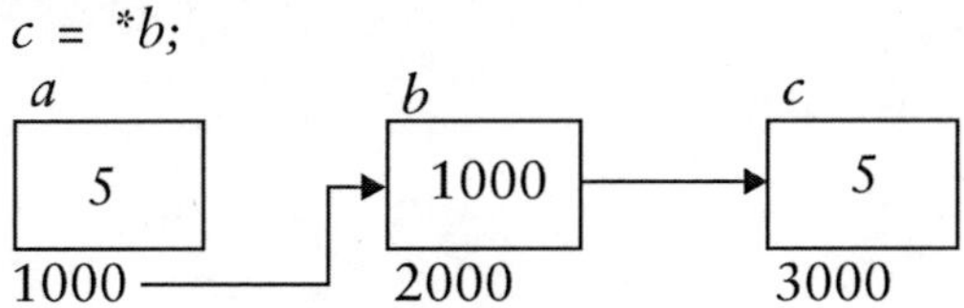

Note: Here in this statement we are storing the value of 'a' to the variable 'c' through Indirection operator. The content of 'b' is the memory address of 'a' and we are taking the value inside that memory address and finally we get the value 5 to 'c'.

Program 9.5 Program to illustrate indirection operator.

```
#include<stdio.h>
#include<conio.h>
void main()
{
  int a,*b,c;
  a=10;
  b=&a;
  c=*b;
  printf("Value of a=%d",a);
  printf("\n Value of b=%u",b);
  printf("\n Value of c=%d",c);
  a=15;
  c=*&a;
  printf("\n Value of c=%d",c);
  getch();
}
```

Output

```
Value of a=10
Value of b=6554
Value of c=10
Value of c=15
```

In the above problem, there is one new statement, c=*&a; this is equivalent to c=*b. In the statement c=*&a, we are taking the content in the memory address of a, simply means the value of a.

The statement

c=*&a ⟹ 10

Similarly

c=*&a=*(&a) =*b=a

9.4 Pointer Expression

We can manipulate pointer variables similar to other memory variables. This enables us to use any of the arithmetic operators along with pointer variables.

Program 9.6 Write a program to illustrate the pointer variables with arithmetic operators.

```
#include<stdio.h>
#include<conio.h>
void main()
{
  int a=5;
  int *b;
  clrscr();
  b=&a;
  printf("%d",*b+10);              ⇨   15
  printf("\n%d",*b+*b);            ⇨   10
  printf("\n%d",*b*(*b));          ⇨   25
  printf("\n%d",*b/(*b));          ⇨   1
  getch();
}
```

Output

```
15
10
25
1
```

-------another program like c = *b+10 → the content of c is....

Note: In the case of division the division operator proceeds the asterisk sign (/*). This is considered as the beginning of a multi-line comment and the statement fails to execute. So it is needed to enclose the second operand within brackets.

Program 9.7 Write a program to illustrate a simple use of incrementing operators in pointers.

```
#include<stdio.h>
#include<conio.h>
void main()
{
  int a=10,*b=&a;
  clrscr();
  printf("\n%d",++*b);  //11
  printf("\n%d",–*b);  // 10
  printf("\n%d",*b+=*b);// 20
```

```
    printf("\n%d",*b*=*b);  // 400
    printf("\n%d",*b/=*b);  //     1
    printf("\n%d",*b-=*b);  //     0
    getch();
}
```

Output

```
11
10
20
400
1
0
```

9.5 Pointer Arithmetic

C pointer is an address, which is a numeric value. Therefore, you can perform arithmetic operations on a pointer just as you can a numeric value. There are four arithmetic operators that can be used on pointers: ++, – –, +, and –.

(a) **Increment:** Let us consider that **ptr** is an integer pointer which points to the address 1000. Assuming 32-bit integers, let us perform the following arithmetic operation on the pointer

```
ptr++
```

Now, after the above operation, the **ptr** will point to the location 1004 because each time ptr is incremented, it will point to the next integer location which is four bytes next to the current location. This operation will move the pointer to next memory location without impacting actual value at the memory location. If **ptr** points to a character whose address is 1000, then above operation will point to the location 1001 because next character will be available at 1001 (character takes 1 byte).

(b) **Decrement:** The same considerations apply to decrementing a pointer, which decreases its value by the number of bytes of its data type.

```
ptr–
```

Now, after the above operation, the **ptr** will point to the location 996 because each time ptr is decremented, it will point to the next integer location which is four bytes previous to the current location. This operation will move the pointer to next memory location without impacting actual value at the memory location. If **ptr** points to a character whose address is 1000, then above operation will point to the location 999 because next character will be available at 999 (character takes 1 byte).

(c) **Adding integer value with pointer:** In C Programming, we can add any integer number to pointer variable. It is perfectly legal in C Programming to add integer to pointer variable. In order to compute the final value we need to use following formulae:

```
final_value = (address) + (number * size of
data type)
```

Example

```
#include<stdio.h>
void main(){
int *ptr=(int *)1000;
ptr=ptr+3;
printf("New Value of ptr : %u",ptr);}
output
New Value of ptr : 1006
```

(d) **Subtracting integer value with pointer:** Suppose we have subtracted "n" from pointer of any data type having initial addess as "init_address" then after subtraction we can write

```
ptr = initial_address - n * (sizeof(data_type))
#include<stdio.h>
void main(){
int *ptr=(int *)1000;
ptr=ptr-3;
printf("New Value of ptr : %u",ptr);
}
```

Output

```
New Value of ptr : 994
```

(e) **Differencing pointers (subtracting pointers):**

```
#include<stdio.h>
void main()
{
```

```
int num , *ptr1 ,*ptr2 ;
ptr1 = &num ;
ptr2 = ptr1 + 2 ;
printf("%d",ptr2 - ptr1);
}
```

Output

```
2
```

Suppose the address of num is 1000. It is assigned to ptr1. The ptr1 is incremented by 2 and assigned to ptr2. Now ptr2 is having the value 1002. The difference gives 2.

(f) Pointer comparison: Two pointers can be compared. It is legal to compare two pointers of different data types.

```
#include<stdio.h>
void main()
{
int *ptr1;
float *ptr2;
ptr1 = (int *)1000;
ptr2 = (float *)2000;
if(ptr2 > ptr1)
  printf("ptr2 is far from ptr1");
}
```

9.6 Pointers and Arrays

An array has a name and the size of the array is mentioned in square brackets. When we declare an array, a base address is located for the array and sufficient amount of continues memory locations are allocated. The base address of the array is represented by the array name.

If we declare *ptr* as an integer pointer, then we can make the pointer *ptr* to point to an array variable *array* by the following assignment:

```
int array[10], *ptr;
ptr = array;
```

This is equal to

```
ptr = array[0];
```

Let us take a simple array program:

Program 9.8 Simple array program without using pointers.

```
#include<stdio.h>
#include<conio.h>
void main()
{
 int a[5]={0,1,2,3,4};
 for(int i=0;i<5;i++)
 printf("%d\n",a[i]);
 getch();
}
```

Output

```
0
1
2
3
4
```

We can re-access the array elements using pointer.

Program 9.9 Simple array program using pointers.

```
#include<stdio.h>
#include<conio.h>
void main()
{
 int a[5]={0,1,2,3,4},i;
 for(i=0;i<5;i++)
 printf("%d\n",*(a+i));
 getch();
}
```

Output

```
0
1
2
3
4
```

We can access array elements using pointer variable also.

Program 9.10 Program to access array elements using pointer variable.

```
#include<stdio.h>
#include<conio.h>
```

```
void main()
{
  int a[5]={0,1,2,3,4},i=0,*p;
  clrscr();
  p=a;
  while(i++<5)
  printf("%d\n",*(p++));
  getch();
  }
```

Output

```
0
1
2
3
4
```

Program 9.11 Another example program to access array elements using pointers.

```
#include<stdio.h>
#include<conio.h>
void main()
{
  int a[5]={0,1,2,3,4},i=0,*p;
  clrscr();
  p=a;
  while(p<&a[5])
  printf("%d\n",*(p++));
  getch();
}
```

Output

```
0
1
2
3
4
```

9.7 Two Dimensional Array Using Pointers

Program 9.12 A simple pointer program in the case of two dimensional array.

```
#include<stdio.h>
#include<conio.h>
```

```
void main()
{
  int a[3][2]={{1,2},{3,4},{5,6}};
  clrscr();
  printf("%u\n",a);
  printf("%u\n",a+1);
  printf("%u\n",*(a+1));
  printf("%u\n",*(a+1)+1);
  printf("%u\n",*(*(a+1)));
  printf("%u\n",*(*(a+1)+1));
  getch();
  }
```

Output

```
65514
65518
65518
65520
3
4
```

```
printf("%u\n",a);  ⇒ Base Address of Array
printf("%u\n",a+1);  ⇒ Base Address of the 2nd Row
printf("%u\n",*(a+1));  ⇒ Address of the 2nd Row
printf("%u\n",*(a+1)+1);  ⇒ Address of 2nd element
                                in 2nd row
printf("%u\n",*(*(a+1)));  ⇒ Content of 1st element
                                in 2nd row
printf("%u\n",*(*(a+1)+1));  ⇒ Content of 2nd
                                element in 2nd row
```

9.8 Pointers and Character Strings

In the case of character variable, we can store a single character in that variable and one byte of space is reserved in memory for that variable. But in the case of a string variable the memory is located in continuous manner as in the case of an array. When we store a word "computer" in a string variable, what is happening in the memory is that totally nine bytes of space is reserved in the memory in continuous locations. Here the word "computer" has only eight digits in size and the 9th space is occupied by a special character named string termination character ('\0').

Program 9.13 Simple program to display a character array.

```
#include<stdio.h>
#include<conio.h>
void main()
{
char a[]="computer";
clrscr();
printf("%s",a);
getch();
}
```

```
computer
```

The above program can also be rearranged by using pointer is given below:

Program 9.14 Simple program to display a character array using pointers.

```
#include<stdio.h>
#include<conio.h>
void main()
{
char *a="computer";
clrscr();
printf("%s",a);
getch();
}
```

```
computer
```

As you know when we mention the array name we are taking the base address of the array rather than its content. We can access the address or content of the array by simply changing the conversion character at the time of printing.

Program 9.15 Program to illustrate the use of pointers for a character array.

```
#include<stdio.h>
#include<conio.h>
void main()
{
char a[]="computer";
char *b;
b=a;
clrscr();
printf("%u",b);
printf("\n%s",b);
getch();
}
```

Output

```
Base Address of array 'a' and the word
'computer'
```

Program 9.16 Program to print each character and address of each character using pointers.

```
#include<stdio.h>
#include<conio.h>
void main()
{
 char *a="computer";
 char *c=a;
 clrscr();
 while(*c!='\0')
 {
 printf("\n%c",*c);
 printf("\n%u",c);
 c++;
 }
 getch();
 }
```

Output

```
c
1000
o
1001
```

```
m
1002
p
1003
u
1004
t
1005
e
1006
r
1007
1008 (This is the address of '\0' which
is the last character stored in array.)
```

In the case of the following statement

```
char a[3][10];
```

we are storing three strings each about maximum ten characters in size including string termination character.

Program 9.17 Draw a flowchart and write a C program to store 15 and 24. Find their sum and then print the result.

```
#include<stdio.h>
#include<conio.h>
void main()
{
  char a[3][10]={"MUMBAI","DELHI","DUBAI"};
  printf("%s %s %s",a,a+1,a+2);
getch();
}
```

Output

```
MUMBAI
DELHI
DUBAI
```

Output with unnecessary storage locations:

In the above Program 9.17, we are reserving totally 30 bytes of memory space for storing the strings including '\0'. But the total used memory is only 21 bytes. This indicates wastage of nine bytes of memory spaces.

M	U	M	B	A	I	\0			
D	E	L	H	I	\0				
C	H	E	N	N	A	I	\0		

If we are not aware about the size of the string and we wish to avoid this problem we can declare the array pointers in another way. This can be discussed by altering the above example slightly.

Program 9.18 Draw a flowchart and write a C program to store 15 and 24. Find their sum and then print the result.

```
#include<stdio.h>
#include<conio.h>
void main()
{
  char *a[3]={“MUMBAI”,”DELHI”,”DUBAI”};
  clrscr();
  printf(“%s %s %s”,*a,*(a+1),*(a+2));
  getch();
}
```

Output

```
MUMBAI
DELHI
DUBAI
```

Output with minimum required memory location:

M	U	M	B	A	I	\0	
D	E	L	H	I	\0		
C	H	E	N	N	A	I	\0

9.9 Pointers and Functions

Pointers allow functions to alter variables outside of their own scope. By passing a pointer to a function we can allow that function to read and write to the data stored in that variable. For example, we want to write a function that swaps the values of two variables. Without pointers this would be practically impossible.

Program 9.19 C program to interchange the values of two variables without using a temporary variable.

```
#include<stdio.h>
void interchange(int *num1,int *num2)
{ int temp;
  temp = *num1;
  *num1 = *num2;
  *num2 = temp;
}
void main() {
  int num1=50,num2=70;
  printf("\n Numbers before swapping\n");
  printf("\nNumber 1 : %d",num1);
  printf("\nNumber 2 : %d",num2);
  interchange(&num1,&num2);
  printf("\n Numbers after swapping\n");
  printf("\nNumber 1 : %d",num1);
  printf("\nNumber 2 : %d",num2);
  }
```

Output

```
Numbers before swapping
Number 1 : 50
Number 2 : 70
Numbers after swapping
Number 1 : 70
Number 2 : 50
```

9.10 Pointers and Structures

Pointers can be accessed along with structures. A pointer variable of structure can be created as below:

```
struct name {
 member1;
 member2;
 .
 .
};
—— Inside function ——
struct name *ptr;
```

Here, the pointer variable of type **struct name** is created.

Structure's member through pointer can be used in two ways:

1. Referencing pointer to another address to access memory
2. Using dynamic memory allocation

Consider an example to access structure's member through pointer.

Program 9.20 C program to access structure member through pointer variable.

```
#include<stdio.h>
struct name{
  int a;
  float b;
};
int main(){
  struct name *ptr,p;
  ptr=&p; /* Referencing pointer to memory address
of p */
  printf("Enter integer: ");
  scanf("%d",&(*ptr).a);
  printf("Enter number: ");
  scanf("%f",&(*ptr).b);
  printf("Displaying: ");
  printf("%d%f",(*ptr).a,(*ptr).b);
  return 0;
}
```

Output

```
Enter integer:10
Enter number:1.2
Displaying:10, 1.2
```

In this example, the pointer variable of type **struct name** is referenced to the address of p. Then, only the structure member through pointer can accessed.

Structure pointer member can also be accessed using -> operator.

```
(*ptr).a is same as ptr->a
(*ptr).b is same as ptr->b
```

9.11 Dynamic Memory Allocation

The exact size of array is unknown untill the compile time, i.e., time when a compier compiles code written in a programming language into a executable form. The size of array you have declared initially can be sometimes insufficient and sometimes more than required. Dynamic memory allocation allows a program to obtain more memory space, while running or to release space when no space is required.

Although, C language inherently does not has any technique to allocated memory dynamically, there are four library functions under "stdlib.h" for dynamic memory allocation.

Function	Use of Function
malloc()	Allocates requested size of bytes and returns a pointer first byte of allocated space.
calloc()	Allocates space for an array elements, initializes to zero and then returns a pointer to memory.
free()	dellocate the previously allocated space.
realloc()	Change the size of previously allocated space.

malloc()

The name malloc stands for "memory allocation". The function malloc() reserves a block of memory of specified size and return a pointer of type void which can be casted into pointer of any form.

Syntax of malloc()

```
ptr=(cast-type*)malloc(byte-size)
```

Here, ***ptr*** is pointer of cast-type. The **malloc**() function returns a pointer to an area of memory with size of byte size. If the space is insufficient, allocation fails and returns NULL pointer.

```
ptr=(int*)malloc(100*sizeof(int));
```

This statement will allocate either 200 or 400 according to size of int 2 or 4 bytes respectively and the pointer points to the address of first byte of memory.

calloc()

The name calloc stands for "contiguous allocation". The only difference between malloc() and calloc() is that, malloc() allocates single block of memory whereas calloc() allocates multiple blocks of memory each of same size and sets all bytes to zero.

Syntax of calloc()

```
ptr=(cast-type*)calloc(n,element-size);
```

This statement will allocate contiguous space in memory for an array of n elements. For example:

```
ptr=(float*)calloc(25,sizeof(float));
```

This statement allocates contiguous space in memory for an array of 25 elements each of size of float, i.e., four bytes.

free()

Dynamically allocated memory with either calloc() or malloc() does not get return on its own. The programmer must use free() explicitly to release space.

syntax of free()

```
free(ptr);
```

This statement cause the space in memory pointer by *ptr* to be deallocated.

Examples of calloc() and malloc()

Write a C program to find sum of n elements entered by user. To perform this program, allocate memory dynamically using malloc() function.

Program 9.21 C program to find the sum of N elements using malloc function.

```
#include<stdio.h>
#include<stdlib.h>
int main(){
  int n,i,*ptr,sum=0;
  printf("Enter number of elements: ");
  scanf("%d",&n);
 ptr=(int*)malloc(n*sizeof(int)); //memory allocated
using malloc
```

```
  if(ptr==NULL)
  {
  printf(“Error! memory not allocated.”);
  exit(0);
  }
  printf(“Enter elements of array: ”);
  for(i=0;i<n;++i)
  {
  scanf(“%d”,ptr+i);
  sum+=*(ptr+i);
  }
  printf(“Sum=%d”,sum);
  free(ptr);
  return 0;
}
```

Output

```
Enter number of elements:3
Enter elements of array:10 20 30
Sum=60
```

Program 9.22 C program to find the sum of N elements using calloc function.

```
#include<stdio.h>
#include<stdlib.h>
int main(){
  int n,i,*ptr,sum=0;
  printf(“Enter number of elements: ”);
  scanf(“%d”,&n);
  ptr=(int*)calloc(n,sizeof(int));
  if(ptr==NULL)
  {
  printf(“Error! memory not allocated.”);
  exit(0);
  }
  printf(“Enter elements of array: ”);
  for(i=0;i<n;++i)
  {
  scanf(“%d”,ptr+i);
```

```
  sum+=*(ptr+i);
  }
  printf("Sum=%d",sum);
  free(ptr);
  return 0;
}
```

Output

```
Enter number of elements:3
Enter elements of array:10 20 30
Sum=60
```

realloc()

If the previously allocated memory is insufficient or more than sufficient. Then, you can change memory size previously allocated using realloc().

Syntax of realloc()

```
ptr=realloc(ptr,newsize);
```

Here, *ptr* is reallocated with size of newsize.

Program 9.23 C program to illustrate realloc function.

```
#include<stdio.h>
#include<stdlib.h>
int main(){
  int *ptr,i,n1,n2;
  printf("Enter size of array: ");
  scanf("%d",&n1);
printf("Enter array elements: ");
ptr=(int*)malloc(n1*sizeof(int));
  for(i=0;i<n1;++i)
  printf("%u\t",ptr+i);
  printf("\nEnter new size of array: ");
  printf("Enter array elements: ");
  scanf("%d",&n2);
  ptr=realloc(ptr,n2);
  printf("The resultant array\n ");
  for(i=0;i<n2;++i)
  printf("%u\t",ptr+i);
  return 0;
}
```

Output

```
Enter size of array:3
Enter array elements:10 20 30
Enter size of new array:4
Enter array elements:40 50 60 70
The resultant array
10
20
30
40
50
60
70
```

9.12 Solved Programs

Program 9.24 C program using pointers to sort a set of 20 numbers and to display the smallest number.

```
#include<stdio.h>
#include<conio.h>
#include<alloc.h>
void main()
{
  int *p,i,j,temp;
  clrscr();
  p=(int *) malloc(20*2);
  if(p==NULL)
  {
      printf("\nMEMORY ALLOCATION UNSUCCESSFUL");
      exit();
  }
  for(i=0;i<20;i++)
  {
      printf("\nENTER NUMBER %d: ",i+1);
      scanf("%d",p+i);
  }
  for(i=0;i<20;i++)
  {
      for(j=0;j<20;j++)
      {
              if(*(p+i)<*(p+j))
              {
```

```
                    temp=*(p+i);
                    *(p+i)=*(p+j);
                    *(p+j)=temp;
            }
        }
    }
    printf("\nTHE SORTED NUMBERS ARE:\n");
    for(i=0;i<20;i++)
        printf("%d\n",*(p+i));
    printf("Smallest number = %d",*(p+0));
getch();
}
```

Output

```
ENTER NUMBER:20 12 13 4 2 1 78 90 56
32 and so on
```

Program 9.25 C program to read N integers and find the sum of squares of all these elements using pointer.

```
#include<stdio.h>
#include<malloc.h>
void main()
{
int i, n, sum = 0;
int *a;
printf("Enter the size of array A \n");
scanf("%d", &n);
a = (int *) malloc(n * sizeof(int));
printf("Enter Elements of the Array \n");
for (i = 0; i < n; i++)
 scanf("%d", a + i);
/* Compute the sum of square of all elements in
the given array */
 for (i = 0; i < n; i++)
 sum = sum + (*(a + i) * *(a+i));
 printf("Sum of squares of all elements in array
= %d\n", sum);
getch();
}
```

Output

```
Enter the size of array A
4
Enter Elements of the Array
1 2 3 4
Sum of squares of all elements in array =30
```

Program 9.26 Write a program using pointers to read in an array of integers and point its element in reverse order.

```
#include<stdio.h>
#include<conio.h>
#define MAX 30
   void main() {
  int size, i, arr[MAX];
  int *ptr;
  clrscr();
  ptr = &arr[0];
  printf("\nEnter the size of array : ");
  scanf("%d", &size);
  printf("\nEnter %d integers into array: ", size);
  for (i = 0; i < size; i++) {
  scanf("%d", ptr);
  ptr++;
  }
  ptr = &arr[size - 1];
 printf("\nElements of array in reverse order are:");
  for (i = size - 1; i >= 0; i–) {
  printf("\nElement%d is %d : ", i, *ptr);
  ptr–;
  }
  getch();
}
```

Output

```
Enter the size of array:5
Enter 5 integers into array:
10
3
2
4
6
```

```
Elements of array in reverse order are:
6
4
2
3
10
```

Program 9.27 Write a program to find the number of characters in a string using pointers.

```
#include<stdio.h>
#include<conio.h>
int Char_Count(char *get_string);
void main()
{char s[50];
int c;
printf("Enter a String: ");
gets(s);
c = Char_Count(s);
printf("\nThe number of characters =%d ",c);
getch();
}
int Char_Count(char *get_string)
{
 int count = 0,i=0;
  while(get_string[i]!='\0')
 { count=count+1;
 i=i+1;
 }
 return count;
 }
```

Output

```
Enter a String:Program
The number of characters = 7
```

Program 9.28 Using pointers, write a C program to add and subtract two matrices of order m x n.

```
#include<stdio.h>
#include<conio.h>
```

```
void main()
{ int *m1=0,*m2=0,*m3,*m4,i,j;
  int row,col,r1,c1;
  int * add(int *m1,int *m2,int row,int col);
 int * subtract(int *m1, int *m2,int row, int col);
  clrscr();
  printf("\nEnter the rows and columns of first
Matrix\n");
scanf("%d%d",&row,&col);
printf("\nEnter the rows and columns of second
Matrix\n");
scanf("%d%d",&r1,&c1);
if(row==r1 &&col==c1){
  printf("\nENTER VALUE FOR THE FIRST Matrix:->");
  m1=(int*) malloc(sizeof(int)*row*col);
  for(i=0;i<row;i++)
  { for(j=0;j<col;j++)
  {scanf("%d",m1+i*col+j);
  }
  }
  printf("\nENTER VALUE FOR THE SECOND Matrix:->");
  m2=(int*) malloc(sizeof(int)*row*col);
  for(i=0;i<row;i++)
  {for(j=0;j<col;j++)
  {scanf("%d",m2+i*col+j);
  }
  }
  m3=(int*) malloc(sizeof(int)*row*col);
  m3=add(m1,m2,row,col);
  printf("\nThe sum of the matrix is\n");
  for(i=0;i<row;i++)
  {
  for(j=0;j<col;j++)
  {printf("%d ",*(m3+i*col+j));
  }
  printf("\n");
  }
  m4=(int*) malloc(sizeof(int)*row*col);
  m4=subtract(m1,m2,row,col);
```

```
  printf("\nThe difference matrix is\n");
  for(i=0;i<row;i++)
  {for(j=0;j<col;j++)
  {printf("%d ",*(m4+i*col+j));
  }
  printf("\n");
  }
}
else
printf("\nThe two matrices cannot be added or
subtracted");
getch();
}
int * add(int *m1,int *m2,int row,int col)
{
  int *m3=(int*) malloc(sizeof(int)*row*col);
  int i,j,k,a1;
  for(i=0;i<row;i++)
  {for(j=0;j<col;j++)
  {a1=*(m1+i*col+j)+*(m2+i*col+j);
  *(m3+i*col+j)=a1;
  }}
  return m3;
}
int * subtract(int *m1,int *m2,int row,int col)
{int *m4=(int*) malloc(sizeof(int)*row*col);
  int i,j,k,a1;
  for(i=0;i<row;i++)
  {for(j=0;j<col;j++)
  {a1=*(m1+i*col+j)-*(m2+i*col+j);
    *(m4+i*col+j)=a1;
  }
  }
  return m4;
}
```

Output

```
Enter the rows and columns of first Matrix
2 2
Enter the rows and columns of second Matrix
2 2
```

```
ENTER VALUE FOR THE FIRST Matrix:->
8 6
10 4
ENTER VALUE FOR THE SECOND Matrix:->
4 3
5 2
The sum of the matrix is
12 9
15 6
The difference matrix is
4 3
5 2
```

9.13 Summary

We have given a detailed description of pointers, pointer arithmetic, pointers and arrays, passing pointers to functions, pointers to structure and dynamic memory allocation functions like malloc(), calloc(), free() and realloc().

9.14 Review Questions

1. What are the uses of pointers?
2. How is a pointer initialized?
3. Explain with examples, the operations on pointers.
4. Explain with suitable examples, how pointers are used as function arguments.
5. Under what conditions two pointer variables can be compared?
6. Explain how a pointer argument is declared within the function definition.
7. What are the practical differences between arrays and pointers?
8. What is meant by dynamic memory allocation?
9. Explain with examples the differences between malloc(), calloc() and realloc() in terms of the functions they perform.
10. Explain static memory allocation and dynamic memory allocation.

CHAPTER 10 Files

10.1 Introduction to Files

Abstractly, a file in C is a stream of characters. By the term *stream*, it represents a standard interface the C language given to the users to work with the wide variety of devices. These devices include disc drives, printers, tape drives, etc. Since all the devices are of different properties, streams which are largely device independent, behave as a consistent interface between the program and devices. The actual device is known as *file*. There are two types of streams that a C language uses: text and binary.

A *text stream* is a sequence of characters and a *binary stream* is a sequence of bytes which has some relationships with the external device. The main difference between a text stream and a binary stream is in how C processes these streams. In a text stream, some character transformation may occur, like a newline character is translated into carriage return/linefeed pair, whereas in a byte stream no character translation occurs.

In C, to work with the file (i.e. any device), we need to associate it with a stream to perform an *open* operation. After opening a file, data can be exchanged by using C standard library file handling functions. We can *close* a file by disassociating the stream from it. So it should be noted that, in C, by associating a stream with the files, we will able to use the file for different operations consistently regardless of its characteristics.

10.2 C File System

The C file system consists of various new *types* and *functions*. One of the important type that relates to the file system is the type **FILE**. The type FILE is a structure type and its structure is defined in *stdio.h* header file. There are number of functions available to work with files, in which *fopen()* and *fclose()* are very important, are defined in *stdio.h* header file.

10.3 File Pointer

To use files in C, we need a *file pointer.* File pointer is a pointer variable to a structure of type **FILE**. Once defined this variable can be used to hold enough information about the file which we want to use that includes the file name, its status and the current position of the file. This variable is also essential for exchanging the data between the file and program. In C, a file pointer variable is declared by

```
FILE *fp;
```

where *FILE* is the structure type defined in C and *fp* is the pointer variable.

10.4 Opening a File

A file must be opened first before we could read or write data. ***fopen()*** function is used to open a file. The *fopen()* function associate a stream with the file to be opened and return a file pointer to the opened file. This function can be used like this

```
FILE *fp = fopen(filename,mode);
```

where *filename* is a valid filename and *mode* is the manner in which the file is to be opened. Below Table shows different values a *mode* can take.

Mode	Use
R	Open an existing text file for opening
W	Create a text file or use existing text file for writing
A	Append to an existing text file or create a new text file
Rb	Open a existing binary file for reading
wb	Create a binary file or use existing binary file for writing
Ab	Append to an existing binary file or create a new binary file
r+	Open a existing text file for read/write
W+	Read data from an existing text file or write data to a new text file
a+	Append or create a text file for read/write
r+b	Open a existing binary file for read/write
W+b	Read data from an existing binary file or write data to a new binary file
a+b	Append or create a binary file for read/write

The following code illustrates the use of *fopen()* function.

```
FILE *fp;
if ((fp = fopen("text.dat", "r")) = = NULL)
{
```

```
    printf("File does not exists or read error");
}
```

Here, the function *fopen()* is used to open the file "text.dat" in "r" (read) mode. If the function is successful it returns a file pointer to the file "text.dat", otherwise a **NULL** pointer will be returned. **NULL** pointer will be returned in the case where the above file does not exist for reading or some read error occurred while reading the above file. The value of **NULL** is defined in *stdio.h*.

10.5 Closing a File

Every file that is opened by a program must be closed in order not to loose the data. The function *fclose()* is used to close a file. The *fclose()* function will disassociate the stream associated with the opened file. The above function can be used like this:

```
fclose(file pointer)
```

where *file pointer* is the pointer variable to a file. For an example,

```
fclose(fp);
```

close the file that is associated with the file pointer *fp*. If the function is successful in closing the file, it will return a zero value, otherwise it returns **EOF** to signifies an error has occurred. The error can be occurred when the disk has been removed permanently or when there is no more space on the disk. The value of **EOF** is defined in *stdio.h*.

Note: If any opened file is not closed explicitly by the user, the C file system automatically closes all the opened files. But, since there is a limit on the number of files that can be opened together, we have to explicitly close one file before opening further.

10.6 File Input Functions

These functions are used to read data from the file to the program. The below are the two common functions used for reading character data from the file.

10.6.1 fgetc Function

The *fgetc()* function returns one character at a time by reading from the file. The function has the following syntax:

```
c = fgetc(fp);
```

where *c* is a character variable used to store the value returned by the *fgetc()* function and *fp* is the file pointer.

10.6.2 fscanf Function

The *fscanf()* function works as same as the *scanf()* function, but only difference is that it reads data from a file. *fscanf()* function reads the data from the file in the way which is specified in the format. The function has the following syntax:

```
fscanf(file pointer,format,variable_list);
```

10.6.3 fgets Function

If *buffer* is a pointer to a character array and *n* is the maximum number of characters to be stored, then *fgets()* function has the following syntax.

```
fgets (buffer, n, input_file)
```

will read an entire line of text (max chars = n) into *buffer* until the newline character or n=max, whichever occurs first. The function places a NULL character after the last character in the buffer. The function will be equal to a NULL if no more data exists.

10.7 File Output Functions

These functions are used to write data to file from the program. The below are the two common functions used for writing character data to a file.

10.7.1 fputc Function

The *fputc()* function is used to write one character at a time to a file at the current position of the pointer in the file. The function has the following syntax:

```
fputc(c,fp);
```

where *c* is the character to be written to the file and *fp* is the file pointer.

10.7.2 fprintf Function

The *fprintf()* works as same as *printf()* function, where only difference is that the function *fprintf()* operates on files. *fprintf()* writes data to the file in a format specified. The function has the following syntax.

```
fprintf(file pointer,format,variable list);
```

10.7.3 fputs Function

If *buffer* is a pointer to a character array and *n* is the maximum number of characters to be stored, then *fputs()* function has the following syntax.

```
fputs (buffer, output_file);
```

writes the characters in *buffer* until a NULL is found. The NULL character is not written to the *output_file*.

10.8 Custom-Access using fseek( ) and ftell( )

We can perform customized read and write operations in a file using the function *fseek()*. This function sets a new position in a file. The function has the following syntax

```
fseek(filepointer,position,origin);
```

where *filepointer* is the pointer variable to the file, *position* is the new position in bytes from the *origin* and *origin* is one of the following keywords defined in C:

Origin	*Keyword*
Beginning of the file	SEEK_SET
Current position	SEEK_CUR
End of the file	SEEK_END

The *fseek()* function returns zero when successful and a nonzero for an error. The following example show how to set a new position in a file 50 bytes from the current position.

```
fseek(fp,50,SEEK_CUR);
```

Another useful function is *ftell()*, which is used to determine the current position of a file. The function has the following syntax.

```
ftell(filepointer);
```

where *filepointer* is pointer variable to a file. On a successful completion of this function, it returns the location of the current position of the file associated with *filepointer*. It will return -1 if it fails.

10.9 Other File Functions

10.9.1 fflush()

We have already seen that a file can be opened for both read and write. However, there will be a situation to flush the contents of the output stream between a read and write or write and read operations. If we did not flush the output stream, we may get data used by the previous operation. Stream flushing is done by the function *fflush()*. The function has the following syntax

```
fflush(filepointer);
```

where *filepointer* is pointer variable to the file. This function clears the stream by writing the buffered data to the file associated with *filepointer*. The *fflush()* function returns zero if successful and EOF for an error.

10.9.2 fread() and fwrite()

If we want to read or write bulk data of any type, other than the usual one byte data, the functions *fread()* and *fwrite()* are useful. The functions have the following syntax

```
fread(buffer,length,count,filepointer);
fwrite(buffer,length,count,filepointer);
```

where *buffer* is a memory region, *length* is the length in bytes of each item, *count* is the number of items that is to be read or write and *filepointer* is the pointer variable to the file. Note that *length* and *count* must be of type *size_t*. The type *size_t* is defined in *stdio.h*

10.9.3 rewind()

The *rewind()* function resets the file position to the beginning of the file. The function has the following syntax.

```
rewind(filepointer);
```

where *filepointer* is the pointer variable to the file.

10.10 C Standard File Streams

Whenever a C program starts its execution, three file streams are automatically opened by the C file system. They are **stdin** (standard input), **stdout** (standard output), and **stderr** (standard error). The above file streams are the standard *file pointers* that are normally associated with the console and these are defined in the *stdio.h*. In the above file pointers **stdin** is used to read from the terminal, and **stdout** and **stderr** are used to write to terminal. The following example describes their use.

fscanf(stdin,"%d",&value); - reads an integer value from the terminal.

fprintf(stdout,"hello world\n"); - prints *hello world* to the terminal.

fprintf(stderr,"Error Reading File"); - prints *Error Reading File* to the terminal.

10.11 Solved Programs

Program 10.1 C Program that counts the number of times the first three letters of the alphabet (A, a, B, b, C, c) occur in a file. Do not distinguish between the lower-case and upper-case letters.

```
#include<stdio.h>
#include<conio.h>
void main()
{
int noa=0,nob=0,noc=0;
FILE *fr;
char fname[20],ch;
clrscr();
printf("\n Enter the source file name: ");
gets(fname);
fr=fopen(fname,"r");
if(fr==NULL)
{
printf("\n error \n");
exit(0);
}
```

```
ch=fgetc(fr);
while(ch!=EOF)
{

if(ch==’A’||ch==’a’)
noa++;
if(ch==’B’||ch==’b’)
nob++;
if(ch==’C’||ch==’c’)
noc++;
ch=fgetc(fr);
}
fclose(fr);
printf(“\n total no of A and a=%d”,noa);
printf(“\n total no of B and b=%d”,nob);
printf(“\n total no of C and c=%d”,noc);
getch();
}
```

Output

```
Enter the source file name:ABC.txt
total no of A and a = 5
total no of B and b = 3
total no of C and c = 2
```

Program 10.2 C program to read in a set of ‘m’ names and their phone numbers. Use a structure variable to store the name and phone number of each customer. Then create a data file.

```
#include<stdio.h>
#include<conio.h>
void main()
{int i, m;
FILE *fptr,*fptr1;
struct phone{
char name[25];
char num[12];
}ph[100];
fptr=fopen(“Hello.txt”,”w”);
```

```
printf(“Enter the limit: ”);
scanf(“%d”,&m);
flushall();
for(i=0;i<m;i++){
printf(“Enter name: ”);
scanf(“%s”,ph[i].name);
printf(“Enter phone number: ”);
scanf(“%s”,ph[i].num);
fprintf (fptr, “Name: %s\n”, ph[i].name);
fprintf (fptr, “Phone Number: %s\n”, ph[i].num);
}
fclose(fptr);
printf(“one file created”);
getch();
}
```

Output

```
Enter the limit:2
Enter name:Adams
Enter phone number:9087654
Enter name:Smith
Enter phone number:3456654
One file created
```

Program 10.3 Write a program to copy the contents of one file to another.

```
#include<stdio.h>
#include<stdlib.h>
void main()
{
  char ch, source_file[20], target_file[20];
  FILE *source, *target;
  printf(“Enter name of file to copy\n”);
  gets(source_file);
  source = fopen(source_file, “r”);
  if( source == NULL )
  {
  printf(“Press any key to exit...\n”);
  exit(EXIT_FAILURE);
  }
```

```
    printf("Enter name of target file\n");
   gets(target_file);
    target = fopen(target_file, "w");
    if( target == NULL )
   {
   fclose(source);
   printf("Press any key to exit...\n");
   exit(EXIT_FAILURE);
   }
   while( ( ch = fgetc(source) ) != EOF )
   fputc(ch, target);
   printf("File copied successfully.\n");
   fclose(source);
   fclose(target);
 }
```

Output

```
Enter name of file to copy
Abc.txt
Enter name of target file
DEF.txt
File copied successfully
```

Program 10.4 Write a program to compare two files and returns '0' if they are equal and '1' if they are not.

```
#include<stdio.h>
void main() {
  FILE *fp1, *fp2;
  int ch1, ch2;
  char fname1[40], fname2[40];
  printf("Enter name of first file :");
  gets(fname1);
  printf("Enter name of second file:");
  gets(fname2);
  fp1 = fopen(fname1, "r");
  fp2 = fopen(fname2, "r");
   if (fp1 == NULL) {
  printf("Cannot open %s for reading ", fname1);
  exit(1);
```

```
} else if (fp2 == NULL) {
printf("Cannot open %s for reading ", fname2);
exit(1);
} else {
ch1 = getc(fp1);
ch2 = getc(fp2);
  while ((ch1 != EOF) && (ch2 != EOF) && (ch1
== ch2)) {
ch1 = getc(fp1);
ch2 = getc(fp2);
}
if (ch1 == ch2){
printf("Files are identical n");
return(0);}
else if (ch1 != ch2){
printf("Files are Not identical n");
return(1);
}
fclose(fp1);
fclose(fp2);
}
}
```

Output

```
Enter name of first file : Abc.txt
Enter name of second file : Def.txt
Files are identical
```

Program 10.5 Write a C program to read a line of text from a file and display the text on the screen.

```
#include<stdio.h>
#include<stdlib.h> /* For exit() function*/
void main()
{
char c[1000];
FILE *fptr;
if ((fptr=fopen("program.txt","r"))==NULL){
printf("Error! opening file");
```

```
  exit(1); /* Program exits if file pointer returns
NULL. */
  }
  fscanf(fptr,"%[^\n]",c);
  printf("Data from file:\n%s",c);
  fclose(fptr);
  getch();
}
```

Output

```
Data from file: C programming
```

Program 10.6 Write a program to append one file to another file.

```
#include<stdio.h>
#include<conio.h>
void main()
{
FILE *fp1,*fp2;
char ch,fname1[20],fname2[20];
printf("\n enter source file name 1");
gets(fname1);
printf("\n enter source file name 2");
gets(fname2);
fp1=fopen(fname1,"r");
fp2=fopen(fname2,"a");
if(fp1==NULL||fp2==NULL)
{
printf("unable to open");
exit(0);
}
do
{
ch=fgetc(fp1);
fputc(ch,fp2);
}
```

```
while(ch!=EOF);
fcloseall();
printf("File appended");
}
```

Output

```
enter source file name 1 Abc.txt
enter source file name 2 Def.txt
File appended
```

10.12 Summary

We have discussed in detail the various types of files, file modes, file operations and functions associated with the processing of files and C standard file streams.

10.13 Review Questions

1. What is the general format of fwrite()?
2. What are the three steps that are followed while accessing a file?
3. Describe the file closing and file opening command in C.
4. What are the characteristics of text and binary files?
5. Explain the concept of file handling.
6. Write a program to create a file, read the file and write on the file.
7. Explain any 10 file handling pre-defined function corresponding syntax.
8. Contrast the use of fread() and fwrite() function with the use of fscanf() and fprintf() function.
9. Summarize the different types that can be specified by the fopen function.

CHAPTER 11 Advanced Topics in C

11.1 Enumeration

Enumeration is a method of grouping a finite set of elements under a name. An *enumeration* is a set of integer constant. So this is also a means of defining a user defined data type. The keyword *enum* is used to declare enumeration types. For example, the declaration

```
enum day{sun, mon, tue, wed, thu, fri, sat};
```

creates a user defined type *enum* day. Then a variable of type *enum day* can be declared like this

```
enum day day_1;
```

The key point to understand about an enumeration is that each of the symbols stands for an integer value. As such, they can be used anywhere that an integer can be used. Each symbol is given a value one greater than the symbol that precedes it. The value of first enumeration symbol is 0.

We can specify the value of one or more of the symbols by using an initializer. This can be done by an equal sign and the integer value. Symbols that appear after an initialization are assigned values greater that the preceding value. For example,

```
enum color{red,green,blue=5,yellow);
```

Here the value of the symbol *red* is 0, *green* is 1, *blue* is 5, and *yellow* is 6. The following shows an example for enumerated type.

```
#include<stdio.h>
enum week{sunday, monday, tuesday, wednesday,
thursday, friday, saturday};
void main(){
  enum week today;
  today=wednesday;
  printf("%d day",today+1);
  }
```

This will produce the following output four day.

11.2 Typedef

C provides a facility called *typedef* for creating new data type names. For example, the declaration

```
typedef int length;
```

makes the name *length* a synonym for *int*. There after the type *length* can be used instead of *int* in declaration as the same way the type *int* can be

```
length len,maxlen;
```

It must be emphasized that a *typedef* declaration does not create a new type in any sense; it merely adds a new name for some existing type. Variables declared this way have exactly the same properties as variables whose declaration are spelled out explicitly. The following gives an example for *typedef*.

```
#include<stdio.h>
#include<string.h>
typedef struct Books {
```

```
  char title[50];
  char author[50];
  char subject[100];
  int book_id;
} Book;
void main() {
  Book book;
  strcpy(book.title, "C Programming");
  strcpy(book.author, "ABC Series");
  strcpy(book.subject, "C Programming
Introduction");
  book.book_id = 6495407;
  printf("Book title : %s\n", book.title);
  printf("Book author : %s\n", book.author);
  printf("Book subject : %s\n", book.subject);
  printf("Book book_id : %d\n", book.book_id);
}
```

This will produce the following result.

```
Book title : C Programming
Book author : ABC Series
Book subject : C Programming Introduction
Book book_id : 6495407
```

11.3 Command Line Arguments

It is possible to pass some values from the command line to your C programs when they are executed. These values are called command line arguments and many times they are important for your program especially when you want to control your program from outside instead of hard coding those values inside the code. The command line arguments are handled using main() function arguments where argc refers to the number of arguments passed, and argv[] is a pointer array which points to each argument passed to the program. Following is a simple example which checks if there is any argument supplied from the command line and take action accordingly:

```
#include<stdio.h>
int main( intargc, char *argv[] )
{
```

```
if(argc == 2)
  {
printf("The argument supplied is %s\n", argv[1]);
  }
else if(argc> 2)
  {
printf("Too many arguments supplied.\n");
  }
else
  {
printf("One argument expected.\n");
  }
}
```

When the above code is compiled and executed with a single argument, it produces the following result.

```
C:>/Tc/a testing
The argument supplied is testing
```

When the above code is compiled and executed with a two arguments, it produces the following result.

```
C:>/Tc/a testing1 testing2
Too many arguments supplied.
```

When the above code is compiled and executed without passing any argument, it produces the following result.

```
C:>/Tc/a
One argument expected
```

It should be noted that argv[0] holds the name of the program itself and argv[1] is a pointer to the first command line argument supplied, and *argv[n] is the last argument. If no arguments are supplied, argc will be one, otherwise and if you pass one argument then *argc* is set at 2.

You pass all the command line arguments separated by a space, but if argument itself has a space then you can pass such arguments by putting them inside double quotes "" or single quotes ''. Let us re-write above example once again where we will print program name and we also pass a command line argument by putting inside double quotes:

```
#include<stdio.h>
int main(intargc, char *argv[])
{
printf("Program name %s\n", argv[0]);

if(argc == 2)
  {
printf("The argument supplied is %s\n", argv[1]);
  }
else if(argc> 2)
  {
printf("Too many arguments supplied.\n");
  }
else
  {
printf("One argument expected.\n");
  }
}
```

When the above code is compiled and executed with a single argument separated by space but inside double quotes, it produces the following result.

```
$./a.out "testing1 testing2"
Program name a
The argument supplied is testing1 testing2
```

11.4 Storage Classes

Every variable in C programming has two properties: type and storage class. Type refers to the data type of variable whether it is character or integer or floating-point value, etc. And storage class determines how long it stays in existence. There are four types of storage class:

1. Automatic
2. Extern
3. Register
4. Static

11.4.1 Automatic

Keyword for automatic variable

```
auto
```

Variables declared inside the function body are automatic by default. These variables are also known as local variables as they are local to the function and don't have meaning outside that function. Since, variable inside a function is automatic by default, keyword auto are rarely used.

11.4.2 Extern

Extern variable can be accessed by any function. They are also known as global variables. Variables declared outside every function are extern variables.

In case of large program, containing more than one file, if the global variable is declared in file 1 and that variable is used in file 2 then, compiler will show error. To solve this problem, keyword ***extern*** is used in file 2 to indicate that, the variable specified is global variable and declared in another file.

Example to demonstrate working of extern variable

```
#include<stdio.h>
void Check();
int a=5;
/* a is global variable because it is outside
every function */
void main()
{
a+=4;
Check();
getch();
}
void Check(){
 ++a;
/* — Variable a is not declared in this
function but, works in any function as they
are global variable —— */
printf("a=%d\n",a);
}
```

Output

```
a=10
```

11.4.3 Register

Keyword to declare register variable

```
register
```

Example of register variable

```
registerint a;
```

Register variables are similar to automatic variable and exists inside that particular function only. If the compiler encounters register variable, it tries to store variable in microprocessor's register rather than in memory. Values stored in register are much faster than that of memory. In case of larger program, variables that are used in loops and function parameters are declared register variables. Since, there are limited number of registers in processor and if it couldn't store the variable in register, it will automatically store it in memory.

11.4.4 Static

The value of static variable persists until the end of the program. A variable can be declared static using keyword: *static*. For example:

```
staticinti;
```

Here, *i*is a static variable.

Example to demonstrate the static variable

```
#include<stdio.h>
void Check();
void main(){
Check();
Check();
Check();
getch();
}
void Check(){
staticint c=0;
printf("%d\t",c);
c+=5;
}
```

Output

```
0    5    10
```

During first function call, it will display 0. Then, during second function call, variable c will not be initialized to 0 again, as it is static variable. So, five is displayed in second function call and ten in third call.

If variable c had been automatic variable, the output would have been:

```
0  0  0
```

11.5 Preprocessor

Preprocessor extends the power of C programming language. Lines that begin with # are called preprocessing directives. The C preprocessor is not a part of the compiler, but is a separate step in the compilation process. A C preprocessor instructs the compiler to do required preprocessing before the actual compilation. It must be the first nonblank character, and for readability, a preprocessor directive should begin in the first column.

Example

```
#define<stdio.h>
#define  PI  3.14
```

These directives tell the C preprocessor to get stdio.h from System Libraries and add the text to the current source file. The next line tells C preprocessor to define the value of PI as 3.14. The following Table 11.1 shows various preprocessor directives and their description.

Table 11.1: Preprocessor Directive and Descriptions

Directive	Description
#define	Substitutes a preprocessor macro.
#include	Inserts a particular header from another file.
#undef	Undefines a preprocessor macro.
#ifdef	Returns true if this macro is defined.
#ifndef	Returns true if this macro is not defined.
#if	Tests if a compile time condition is true.

#else	The alternative for #if.
#elif	#else and #if in one statement.
#endif	Ends preprocessor conditional.
#error	Prints error message on stderr.
#pragma	Issues special commands to the compiler, using a standardized method.

(a) #define: This directive is also called as Macro substitution directive.

Syntax:

```
#define<Macro_constant> [(<Para1>, <Para2>,...)]
<Token_string>
[] indicates optional term.
```

Task of macro substitution directive is to replace the identifier with corresponding Token_string. For example:

```
#include <stdio.h>
#define pie 3.14
void main() {
float r=3,area;
area = 3 * r * pie;
printf("%f",area);
}
```

In the above C code we have defined a macro constant pie. Before the starting of actual compilation an intermediate is formed which is:

```
#include<stdio.h>
void main() {
float r=3,area;
area = 3 *r * 3.14;
printf("%f",area);
}
```

(b) #include

Syntax:

```
#include<filename>
```

or

```
#include "filename"
```

Task of include directive is to include or import any type file. There are two forms of include directive.

1. #include<filename>: This statement will search the file in include directory (Default location of include directory is c:\tc\include). If that file is present then #include statement is replaced by content of file. If that file is not present then it will cause of compilation error. The following shows an example.

```
#include<stdio.h>
#include<conio.h>
void main(){
clrscr();
printf("HOW large is this file?");
getch();
}
```

2. #include "filename": This statement will first search the given file any current working directory and if it is not present then it will search include directory if it is also not present there then it will cause of compilation error, unable to open the file. If that file is present then include statement is replaced by content of file.

Example

If file is present in the current working directory. Suppose my current working directory is c:\tc\bin

```
//c:\tc\bin\one.c
int a=5;
int b=10;
//c:\tc\bin\two.c
#include"stdio.h"
#include"one.c"
void main(){
 printf("a=%d b=%d",a,b);
 }
```

(c) #if,#else and #endif: It is conditional compilation directive. That is if condition is true then it will compile the C programming code otherwise it will compile the c code in else directive. #endif shows the end of condition.

Example Program

```
#include<stdio.h>
#define a 100
int main()
{
  #if (a==100)
  printf("The value of A is 100");
  #else
  printf("The value of a is not equal to 100");
  #endif
  return 0;
}
```

Output

```
The value of A is 100
```

The "If" clause statement is included in source file if given condition is true. Otherwise, else clause statement is included in source file for compilation and execution.

(d) #elif: Processor directive #elif is part of #if directive. It will execute only if it's just previous constant expression of #if or #elif is zero.

Example Program

```
#include<stdio.h>
void main(){
  #if(!5>=5)
  int a=5;
  #elif -1
  int a=10;
  #else
  int a=15;
  #endif
  printf("%d",a);
}
```

Output

```
10
```

Explanation: Consider on the expression: !5 >= 5

= 0 >= 5

= 0

So #if is false. Now it will execute first #ielif directive.

(e) **#ifdef:** Directive #ifdef is very similar to #if except its conditional statement which is identifier instead of a constant expression. Identifier may a macro constant or global identifier. It only checks identifier has been defied or not. It doesn't care what the value of identifier is. If identifier has been defined then it executes #ifdef body otherwise it executes the body of #else directive.

Example Program

```
#include<stdio.h>
#define ABC 25
#define PQR "Exact Help"
void main(){
  int num = 3;
  #ifdef ABC
  printf("%d",ABC * ABC);
  #else
  printf("%s",PQR);
  #endif
}
```

Output

```
625
```

Explanation: Since macro constant ABC has defined so #ifdef condition is true. Hence, the statements in #ifdef will be executed.

(f) **#ifndef:** Directive #ifndef is just opposite to the directive #ifdef. In this case if identifier has not defined then #ifndef is true and if identifier has defined then #ifndef condition will false.

Example Program

```
#include<stdio.h>
#define int 'A'
void main(){
  char num = int;
  #ifndef int
  printf("Please define int");
  #else
```

```
  printf("%d",int);
  #endif
}
```

Output

```
65
```

Explanation: Macro constant int has been defined so #else directive will execute.

(g) **#undef:** Directive #undef is used to undefine any macro constants except global identifiers. It is useful when we want to redefined any macro constants.

Example Program

```
#include<stdio.h>
#define ABC 25
#ifdef ABC
#undef ABC
#define ABC 50
#else
#define ABC 100
#endif
void main(){
  printf("%d",ABC);
}
```

Output

```
50
```

Explanation: Since macro constant ABC has already defined. So #ifdef condition is true. Directive #undef will undefined the macro constant ABC but #define will again define.

(h) **#error:** If compiler compiles this line then it shows a compiler fatal error, i.e. it only issue an error message.

Example Program

```
#include<stdio.h>
#ifndef __MATH_H
#error First include then compile
#else
int main(){
```

```
    float a,b=25;
    a=sqrt(b);
    printf("%f",a);
    return 0;
  }
  #endif
```

Output

```
Output: compiler error —> Error directive:First
include then compile
```

(i) **#pragma:** Pragma is implementation specific directive, i.e. each pragma directive has different implementation rule and use. There are many type of pragma directive and varies from one compiler to another compiler. If compiler does not recognize particular pragma then it simply ignore that pragma statement without showing any error or warning message and execute the whole program assuming this pragma statement is not present. Consider the following example.

Example Program

```
#include<stdio.h>
#pragma world
void main(){
 printf("C is powerful language ");
 }
```

Output

```
C is powerful language
```

Since #pragma world is unknown for C compiler so it will ignore this directive without showing any error or warning message and execute the whole program assuming #pragma world statement is not present.

```
#pragma startup and #pragma exit
```

Syntax:

```
#pragma startup [priority]
#pragma exit [priority]
```

where priority is optional integral number. For user priority varies from 64 to 255, for c libraries priority varies from 0 to 63 and default priority is 100.

#pragma startup always execute the function before the main function. #pragma exit always execute the function after the main function. Function declaration of must be before startup and exit pragma directives and function must not take any argument and return void. If more than one startup directive then priority decides which will execute first.

```
startup:
```

Lower value: Higher priority, i.e. functions will execute first. If more than one exit directive then priority decides which will execute first.

```
exit:
```

Higher value: Higher priority, i.e. functions will execute first. Consider the following example.

Example Program

```
void india();
void usa() ;
#pragma startup india 105
#pragma startup usa
#pragma exit usa
#pragma exit india 105
void main(){
printf("\nI am in main");
getch();
}
void india(){
printf("\nI am in india");
getch();
}
void usa(){
printf("\nI am in usa");
getch();
}
```

Output

```
I am in usa
I am in india
I am in main
I am in india
I am in usa
```

Explanation: In the above program there are two startup directives which will execute before the main function.

Function name india has priority 105.

Function name usa has priority 100 (default).

So usa function will execute first than india function and above program there are two exit directive which will execute after the main function.

Function name india has priority 105.

Function name usa has priority 100 (default).

So india function will execute first than usa function.

11.6 Macros

A macro is a name given to a block of C statements as a preprocessor directive. Being a preprocessor, the block of code is communicated to the compiler before entering into the actual coding (main () function). A macro is defined with the preprocessor directive, #define.

The advantage of using macro is the execution speed of the program fragment. When the actual code is to be used, it can be substituted by the name of the macro. The same block of statements, on the other hand, need to be repeatedly hard coded as and when required.

The disadvantage of the macro is the size of the program. The reason is, the preprocessor will replace all the macros in the program by its real definition prior to the compilation process of the program.

11.6.1 Macros with Argument

Preprocessing directive #define can be used to write macro definitions with parameters with the following syntax.

```
#define identifier(identifier 1,.....identifier n)
token_string
```

Again, the token string is optional but, are used in almost every case. Let us consider an example of macro definition with argument.

Example

```
#define area(r) (3.1415*(r)*(r))
```

Here, the argument passed is *r*. Every time the program encounters area(argument), it will be replace by (3.1415*(argument)*(argument)). Suppose, we passed (r1+2) as argument then, it expands as below:

```
area(r1+2) expands to (3.1415*(r1+2)*(r1+2))
```

Example program to find the area of a circle

```
#include<stdio.h>
#define PI 3.1415
#define area(r) (PI*(r)*(r))
int main(){
  int radius;
  float area;
  printf("Enter the radius: ");
  scanf("%d",&radius);
  area=area(radius);
  printf("Area=%.2f",area);
  return 0;
}
```

Output

```
Enter the radius: 4
Area=50.26
```

11.6.2 Pre-defined Macros

ANSI C defines a number of macros. Although each one is available for use in programming, the predefined macros should not be directly modified. The following Table 11.2 shows a list of pre-defined macros.

Pre-defined macro	Value
__DATE__	String containing the current date
__FILE__	String containing the file name
__LINE__	Integer representing the current line number
__STDC__	If follows ANSI standard C, then value is a non-zero integer
__TIME__	String containing the current date

Example Program

```
#include<stdio.h>
int main(){
   printf("Current  date:  %s\n",__DATE__);   //
calculate the current date
   printf("Current  time:  %s\n",__TIME__);   //
calculate the current time
  return 0;
}
```

Output

```
Current date: Dec 1 2015
Current time: 02:21:48
```

11.7 Solved Programs

Program 11.1 C Program that will receive a file name and a line of text as command line arguments and write the text to the file.

```
#include<stdio.h>
void main(int argc, char *argv[])
{
  FILE *fp;
  int i;
  char word[20];
  fp=fopen(argv[1], "w"); /* open file with name
argv[1] */
  printf("\n No. of arguments in command line =
%d\n",argc);
  for(i=2;i<argc;i++)
      fprintf(fp,"%s",argv[i]);  /*  write  to  file
argv[1] */
  fclose(fp);
  /* writing the contents of the file to the screen
*/
  printf("Contents of %s file\n\n", argv[1]);
  fp=fopen(argv[1],"r");
  for(i=2;i<argc;i++)
  {
```

```
        fscanf(fp,"%s",word);
        printf("%s  ",word);
    }
    fclose(fp);}
```

Output

```
C:>Test> Copyfile ABC.txt DEF.txt
No. of arguments in command line =3
Contents of DEF.txt
Apple
Orange
```

Program 11.2 Write a nested macro that gives the minimum of three values.

```
#include<stdio.h>
#include<conio.h>
#define min(a,b)  ((a>b)?b:a)
#define minthree(a,b,c)  (min(min(a,b),c))
void main()
{
int x,y,z,w;
clrscr();
printf("enter three numbers :\n");
scanf("%d%d%d",&x,&y,&w);
z=minthree(x,y,w);
printf("Minimum of three value is %d",z);
getch();
}
```

Output

```
Enter three numbers : 1 2 3
Minimum of three value is 1
```

11.8 Summary

In this chapter, we have covered advanced topics like enumerations, typedefs, command line arguments and various storage classes like automatic, extern, register and static. This chapter has also covered preprocessor directives and macros.

11.9 Review Questions

1. What is the purpose of typedef?
2. Write short notes on enumerated data types?
3. What are command line arguments?
4. Briefly explain various storage classes in c.
5. Explain preprocessors in c.
6. What are macros?
7. What are the advantages and disadvantages of macros?
8. Discuss on different categories of C preprocessor.